BI
VOICES

BIBLE VOICES

MEDITATIONS FROM CREATION TO APOCALYPSE

Ideal for busy speakers in churches and schools

ANTHONY GEERING

Text copyright © Anthony Geering 2000
The author asserts the moral right
to be identified as the author of this work

Published by
The Bible Reading Fellowship
Peter's Way, Sandy Lane West
Oxford OX4 6HG
ISBN 1 84101 145 2

First published 2000
10 9 8 7 6 5 4 3 2 1 0

Acknowledgments
Unless otherwise stated, scripture quotations are taken from
The Revised Standard Version of the Bible, copyright © 1946, 1952,
1971 by the Division of Christian Education of the National Council
of the Churches of Christ in the United States of America, and are
used by permission. All rights reserved.

A catalogue record for this book is available from the British Library

Printed and bound in Great Britain by
Omnia Books Limited, Glasgow

PREFACE

It almost goes without saying that the Bible is rich in wonderful stories, powerful characters and the most significant themes of love, life and death. Nothing can compare with the original.

This collection of monologues (which can also be used as meditations) is simply a different way into the Bible. It may serve as an introduction for those scared off by a 'holy' book. It may encourage others to look again at familiar passages or ideas. It may help still others to discover something of the breadth and warmth of both Jewish and Christian scriptures.

I hope that many of these monologues will speak for themselves. They do demand a prior knowledge of the Bible passage, however superficial, but seek to enhance that knowledge, to put flesh on the characters.

They have been written in the first instance for all-age worship, for older teenagers, for ecumenical gatherings, even (where the story is very familiar) as illustrations for after-dinner speeches for audiences as varied as Young Farmers or golf clubs! They are offered also to individuals for reflection and enjoyment.

Humour has always played a large part in communicating important or serious messages. Quite a few of the monologues play on a sense of the ridiculous or plain quirky. Others try to come at a situation or an individual's involvement more soberly, usually from an acute angle to arrest the reader's or listener's attention.

The scripts have grown out of a lively love of the Bible. They have been tested by inventive and imaginative people before a supportive yet critical congregation.

Anthony Geering

CONTENTS

USING THIS BOOK

Shape and contents

A broad sweep of Bible characters is here, as the subtitle of the book indicates. Some biblical characters and events are more attractive or compelling than others, and so there are obvious gaps for anyone seeking a comprehensive survey of the Bible 'from creation to apocalypse'.

Each of the fifty monologues stands or falls by its own merits, but as a collection, they offer a broad survey of the Bible. It is therefore possible to read the book as a unity, from beginning to end. This will be to discover something of the Bible as a series of books that steadily (if unevenly from a literary point of view) unfolds the great story of God's loving purpose.

Each monologue is prefaced with explanatory notes which also implicitly try to provide a narrative thread between monologues.

The monologues

Monologues are verbal rather than visual theatre. Their impact when performed in public is immediate: the actor only gets one chance. It is their instancy that makes them a useful dramatic form. They are compact and easily rehearsed. They are also designed for individual use with the Bible, when it is hoped that they will have a more enduring effect. Some of the monologues are set in the characters' own time. Others are made to be contemporary, largely to increase their impact and applicability. This is indicated in the text.

The word 'monologue' implies that the script is a very personal speech. It suggests that we are privy to innermost thoughts and feelings.

These biblical monologues are also a way of focusing on particular individuals, perhaps not central characters, and to ponder creatively on their role in the overall story.

Practical help

Each monologue is prefaced by three 'flashpoint' sections. The first comes under the main heading of the name of the biblical character or event, and gives a Bible reference and a resumé of the passage and its intention. It is introductory.

The second section is usually more detailed and offers some background to the Bible passage, possible lines for discussion, and, often, why the monologue has been conceived in a particular way. It is headed 'For further reflection or discussion'. This section also needs to be employed before a monologue is used. If it is to illustrate a sermon or introduce a discussion, the monologue itself needs a proper introduction. It needs to be intelligently understood and confidently delivered.

The final section is headed 'Suggestions for staging'. Mostly practical, it sometimes adds some hints about the purpose of the monologue. The staging is intended to be simplicity itself. It is perfectly possible to read the script after the briefest introduction and then expand on it. That might happen within a sermon.

More detailed scenery and props are fun but unnecessary. However, the suggestions do cover a more elaborate presentation, perhaps within an all-age act of worship, or as a theme setter for discussion groups.

The question of costuming is one that needs more consideration. Monologues are minimalist drama, and token costuming can reinforce their spontaneity and impact; for example, through appropriate headwear —a Near Eastern headcloth and cord, a cardboard soldier's helmet, or a shawl. These, along with simple props such as a fishing net, basket or sword, can provide sufficient 'colour' to suggest character and setting. Alternatively, full authenticity might be desired. Nowadays, costume hire is available in most modest-sized towns. Friendly theatre stage managers or amateur drama groups can offer advice or help. Accuracy can be checked in reference libraries, and it is often children's illustrated history books that are most helpful. Hints about dressing specific characters have been included in the text, with more descriptive detail for difficult costumes.

It may at first appear daunting for an actor to speak as a tree or an animal. These and all the monologues require some audience preparation. Many groups nowadays, and certainly young people in school assemblies, are attuned to such dramatic devices. Presenters should be aware of sensitivities in offering this way of raising deep issues of God and creature, life and death. It should be stressed that the Bible uses humour, talking animals, gimmicks and shock tactics.

Jesus is the master wordsmith and through his stories (which cannot be improved upon) he gives us wonderful spiritual pictures and messages that jolt and then go on quietly shaking us.

For reference

Proper names of main biblical characters and places are listed in an index. A separate subject index of themes and festivals is also provided to help you to choose the right monologue to illustrate a sermon, initiate a discussion or ignite an assembly. The numbers refer to monologues rather than pages.

Bible study

The monologues can be a personal resource. They are not exclusively designed for wider groups. It is hoped that by reading through them and pursuing other hints and references, individuals will be drawn to read the passage and explore the Bible context further.

The Bible provides counsel, consolation and challenge. It becomes for each of us a living word as God's voice speaks.

Bible versions

References and quotations in this book are from the Revised Standard Version. There are many other versions nowadays. Each can offer distinctive emphases on most familiar passages. If you are new to Bible reading and study, be sure to find a translation that looks and feels comfortable and contemporary.

I

GOD

Genesis 1 tells the story of creation. How did everything begin? This opening chapter of the Bible shows creation as a sort of conversation that begins within the Godhead, spreads out and becomes unstoppable.

For further reflection or discussion

This is the first of two creation stories in the book of Genesis. The focus is firmly on planet Earth. It is only on the third day of creation, when the dry land of the Earth is revealed, that the repetitive refrain 'And God saw that it was good' begins. The story unfolds in a way that underlines the orderliness of creation. God works to a progressive plan and his job satisfaction is obvious. Thus humankind is made 'after our likeness', both male and female (as verse 27 makes clear in balanced repetition). The gift of dominion over every living thing is not a licence to exploit, rather a delegation of responsibility.

Unlike other ancient peoples, the Hebrews did not believe that pre-existent matter was the stuff of creation and even of gods. Creation is by the word of God:

By the word of the Lord the heavens were made, and all their host by the breath of his mouth… For he spoke, and it came to be; he commanded, and it stood forth (Psalm 33:6, 9).

Christ is described as the pre-existent Word in the prologue of John's Gospel. As *the Word* of God, he is more than speech. He is God in action who makes, reveals, redeems. Such activity moves beyond communication to communion. The account of God's making and humanity's breaking of this communion is told as a tragic but ultimately glorious love story, unfolding throughout the Bible.

The 'I became Us' of the monologue is an attempt to describe the mystery that Christians call the Trinity. When the Word is made flesh, the Godhead can never be the same again. The fault of Adam has, by God's grace, brought us into the intimacy of that perfect union. How vulnerable God has become through creation!

Small wonder he might think, 'No way!'

Suggestions for staging

God speaks.

The setting is plain.

The voice of God should be amplified and the actor should not appear.

The script is read very slowly as commentary to pictures on an overhead projector.

Choice of images could include, in this order: waves on a seashore, a clock face, animal life, two lovers kissing, a war scene, constellations and a bowl of fruit.

THE PROLOGUE

There was a moment, probably the very first moment ever or certainly the second, when I thought, 'No way!'

But it was already too late. The trouble with inventing Time is that it cannot then be denied. Whatever will happen may have happened already somewhere. There is no retreat into Eternity.

And having the thought in the first place brought words into being.

Then, with the Word begotten, there was love and communion to enjoy and somehow the need to put flesh on the words. To delight in contrasts, textures, fragrance. To face up to differences, rejection, fears. Infinity was invaded and would never be the same again.

It had been peaceful, but it was lonely. Now love had an object.

I became Us and I spoke and I saw that everything, just then, was good, very good.

2

THE FALL

Genesis 3:1–9. The story of the Fall is not just about disobedience on humanity's part, nor even the desire for power or wisdom. It is mainly a fall from trust. Relationships carry responsibilities.

For further reflection or discussion

For a people whose history included desert wanderings, gardens figure prominently in Jewish stories as places of refuge, rest and delight. Eden means 'delight'. Gardens are the opposite of wilderness (Isaiah 51:3).

The Song of Songs is a series of love poems set, as it were, in a garden where innocence and beauty are restored and enjoyed. It is to a garden that Jesus retreats after the last supper (John 18:1). It is in a garden that Mary Magdalene finds him on Easter morning (John 19:41). It is in a garden city, the new Jerusalem, that the tree of life flourishes at the end of time (Revelation 22:2).

In Eden, the two trees (Genesis 2:9) symbolize God's attributes of eternal life and wisdom. Eden is where God is. It is a place of innocence, a haven where problems such as pain, fear, loneliness, lovelessness and death do not exist.

But the potential for mortality and for evil is present in the garden. The knowledge is there: it is God's, to know right from wrong. Why, then, is the fruit dangled before Adam and Eve? Because otherwise they would not be truly free.

The problem is, therefore, not that God forbids humans freedom or control of their destiny or the chance to enquire and discover more about their environment. The story is about rejected partnership, broken trust and 'power over'—themes that remain contemporary.

The tree is allowed here to speak, to highlight primeval innocence. Yet there is something insubstantial and unconvincing about such innocence. It is almost selfish. The thought intrudes that the Fall, even if not meant, is none the less inevitable. Something to do with divine discontent...

Finally, Eden is perceived as an actual place on (and of) Earth. The hope can always exist that there may be a way back.

Suggestions for staging

The setting is the garden of Eden and the main character is the Tree of the Knowledge of Good and Evil.

The actor is dressed as a tree, in green and brown, and carries leafy twigs hung with fruits. Adam and Eve stand before him. They can be dressed in skin-coloured tights and T-shirts.

The monologue is delivered in a slightly gushing, naïve voice that gradually becomes more querulous.

At the end of the monologue there is a pause. Then Adam and Eve slowly and deliberately reach out and pick a fruit, and each takes a bite from the other's.

IGNORANCE IS BLISS

Tree of the Knowledge of Good and Evil, you say? Me?

No, I'm afraid I have no idea what you're talking about. But very kind of you to say so.

I just grow here in the middle of the Garden, looking lovely and bearing fruit. Hadn't really thought of anything else. It's the Lord God you want. Talk to him. He'll tell you whatever it is you want to know. He's so terribly clever. He's the Gardener. For instance, look at my fruit. Brilliant, hey?

No, it's not an apple, actually. Not pear, pomegranate, persimmon, pineapple or papaya. Rather better than a combination of those.

As I say, God's your man. I don't do the knowledge stuff. I just enjoy being a tree. So whatever it is you want to know, please don't involve me. What you other creatures do is your business. Or God's. Nothing to do with me, my friends. You just let me alone to stand here at the heart of the Garden looking ravishing. I'll sap, I'll spread, I'll fruit. But I won't be responsible for others. Make your own choices; I'm just an innocent bystander.

To be absolutely frank, for the life of me I can't see why God let you in here, wanting to complicate matters. Why can't you just leave things alone? Everything in the Garden is lovely.

3
CAIN AND ABEL

Genesis 4:2–16. The story of Cain and Abel grapples with powerful human emotions. Uncontrollable passions are often inflicted on those closest to us. Issues of rebellion, jealousy and conflict are raised by Cain's famous question of God, 'Am I my brother's keeper?'

For further reflection or discussion

Cain reads like a peevish young man. He is quick to excuse and justify himself, but really the issues are more fundamental. The story suggests that the problem is not the tension between farmers and semi-nomads, not God's apparent favouritism of one way of life over another, but Cain's attitude and relationship to God.

'If you do well, will you not be accepted? And if you do not do well, sin is crouching at the door; its desire is for you, but you must master it' (v. 7).

Even yet, God is seeking damage limitation of humanity's rejection of him. The child of Adam and Eve will move rebellion a stage further with fratricide.

A secondary theme of tension between two conflicting ways of life has resonances with today's world. Australian aborigines or Kalahari tribesmen face the loss of a traditional way of life as settlers spread. The Bible expresses this tension in terms of Abel's blood crying from the ground. Alienation from God or fellow human being, it is suggested, is also alienation from the earth and its resources.

Cain recognizes this:

'My punishment is greater than I can bear. Behold, thou hast driven me this day away from the ground; and from thy face I shall be hidden' (vv. 13–14).

In the monologue, it is Cain's initial peevishness that remains the focus. Here he is made to enumerate the three standard complaints of a child: it's not fair; it's not my fault; I didn't ask to be born.

And here begins the well-worn excuse of humanity through the ages—blame God.

Suggestions for staging

In the monologue, Cain may use the mannerisms of a modern courtroom, conducting his own defence, perhaps speaking from a lectern or haranguing a 'jury' (the audience).

COUNSEL FOR THE DEFENCE

My Lord, if it please the court, I would like to make a statement. I realize that this is irregular but I cite unusual and exceptional circumstances and ask for the court's indulgence.

I have pleaded not guilty to the murder of my brother. This I do for the following three reasons. Firstly, it's not fair. My brother Abel was given the job of shepherd, whereas I was given that of market gardener. Nowhere was it written that his job should be more favoured than mine. Yet it was so. I find this incomprehensible and inexcusable. Why should I be penalized for having the wrong occupation?

Secondly, it's not my fault. Oh, I accept the lesser charge of manslaughter. It would be hard to refute, with my brother's blood crying out from the ground. But no one ever took the trouble to explain to me the distinction between being alive and being dead. I learnt from my parents the difference between being right and being wrong. But I had never seen death. How could I know it to be so irrefutably final or life so infinitely fragile? I wanted to hurt my brother, not destroy him. I should have been told we are not immortal, that you only get one chance.

Thirdly, I didn't ask to be here anyway. I cannot be held responsible for my existence. No more than I can be held responsible for my prejudices, emotions and physical strengths. I cannot be brought into being and then made liable for the manufacturer's design faults.

In conclusion, I would remind the court, I am already punished with the mark of an outcast. I ask you therefore to consider carefully whether my very existence is fair, blameworthy, or self-chosen. The one who should be on trial in this court, my Lord, with the greatest respect, is *you*.

4
MRS NOAH

Genesis 8:8. God's punishment of a wicked world is seen in a vast flood and he begins to work through a faithful few. Their mark is constancy when things look hopeless.

For further reflection or discussion

Water is a powerful sign in the Bible. Its properties to cleanse, renew and sustain life are vividly apparent to desert people, to those of Mesopotamia ('the land between two rivers'), and to those near the Nile and Jordan rivers. Because it was believed that in creation God had gathered the waters together and formed dry land, so the story of Noah was a repetition—a recreation of the world. The world on which Noah steps ashore is completely new. There is a fresh start.

After the flood, God sets a sign of his new promise in the sky. It is a rainbow.

Storms and rain are God's cataclysmic judgment on a world gone rotten. Sunshine marks restoration and a new life. The rainbow is a part of each. It is a bridge from earth to heaven—God reaching out to touch humanity, and humanity reaching out to touch God.

Although Noah's story is superficially similar to the Gilgamesh Epic from Babylonia, its intention is to show that this is not the gods' caprice but God's judgment. Only Noah is in a true and proper (that is, right-eous) relationship with God.

The story of Noah and the flood is one of the most vivid in the Biblical narrative. Here the harassed ark-wife has her say. It is hard to imagine the domestic trial of life on a floating zoo measuring some 150 metres long, 25 broad and 15 high.

Suggestions for staging

The setting is Noah's ark and the character is Noah's wife.

Fun can be had making an *ad hoc* ark and using people with animal masks for a colourful scene.

Mrs Noah should be just visible through the window of the ark. A large cardboard packing case would help to create this impression.

The recorded trumpeting of an elephant, or even two people dressed as a 'pantomime elephant', will enhance the presentation, particularly of the ending. The cardboard scenery could be pushed over to reveal her dilemma.

S.O.S.

Dear Anyone,
This is our thirty-ninth day afloat and my fifteenth message in a bottle. If only the rain would stop. I promise never to grumble about the weather again.

Dear Anyone,
Yes, it has to be that. Anyone.

Can there be anyone out there after all this rain and all this time? I wish I'd taken Noah more seriously now—packed a few more novels and my knitting. Don't suppose I'll ever finish that sweater for Japheth now.

Dear Anyone,
Anyone from the human race. Anyone else to talk to apart from these moaning minnies. They do nothing. Just sit around complaining about what's run out next. We're totally out of bananas and mulberry leaves. Down to our last few sacks of corn, but (surprise, surprise!) still got plenty of barrels of beer. Oh, well, we can die merry, I suppose.

Dear Anyone,
You must be in a boat like us. Have you seen even the tip of a mountain? Did you rescue insects as well, and if you did, can I swat a few in here? They give me the creeps, these big orange spiders. And how is your smell? Can't be worse than ours. And tell me this, how come all the fish got saved but only two of everything else? Please, no pun about souls.

Dear Anyone,
I'm running out of pencil and I've smashed the last bottle, so now for the crucial message. If this carrier pigeon reaches you, please come urgently to large ark. I am trapped in the Elephant House. No one is answering, and one of the beasts is standing on my foot.

Lily Noah (Mrs)

5
ABRAHAM

Genesis 12:1–4. Abraham is chosen by God to be the father of a great nation. He is prepared to leave family behind and obey the summons.

For further reflection or discussion

At the time of Abraham, two thousand years before Christ, settled city states existed in Mesopotamia, the land around the rivers Tigris and Euphrates. At the same time, important migrations were producing new kingdoms and influences in the region. Abraham and his family were caught in this migratory melée of Amorites from Arabia, Hurrians from Armenia and Hittites from Turkey. As the letter to the Hebrews says, '(Abraham) went out, not knowing where he was to go' (Hebrews 11:8).

Abraham is neither refugee nor pioneer, but visionary. In the midst of lands that are in social and political flux, he leads out his people. God has isolated this one man who is obedient and faithful, and childless, to be the righteous patriarch of Israel.

Suggestions for staging

The monologue can be delivered by the Public Relations man of the Caravan Company. He is in modern dress, a bit flash, and is perhaps dictating the letter to a secretary.

GO WEST, YOUNG MAN!

Dear Mr Abram,

Thank you for your recent enquiry about our Pioneers' Trail. We have much pleasure in enclosing our latest brochure entitled 'Fertile Crescent' for your perusal.

May we offer the following preliminary points prompted by our long experience in the travel industry? We would wish to inform you that joining one of our caravans can be a hazardous adventure. In particular, we must disclaim at the outset any responsibility or liability for the action of hostile tribesmen, or Act of God.

Potential dangers lurk not merely on the lonelier portions of the trail but in more populated regions, such as the infamous Cities of the Plain. Should you be considering travelling *en famille*, may we emphasize that you should certainly upgrade to our Armed Escort Service. Different sorts of problems may be encountered by your womenfolk, not least Egyptian harem-catchers.

We are sure that you have weighed such disadvantages of trekking west against the many advantages to which our satisfied clients can attest (see our brochure). Fortunes are to be made in the thinly settled lands on the western seaboard or in the Nile Delta region. We understand your need to expand as a successful wandering herdsman and that you have significantly outgrown available land in Mesopotamia, most recently in Haran. With our organization, a resourceful, driving personality such as your good self will discover lands of plenty, lands of opportunity. Trust yourself to us, dear Mr Abram. Our teamwork and success rates are second to none.

We look forward to your esteemed custom. Our agent in Ur of the Chaldees will be happy to proffer further advice and assistance. Remember our motto, 'The desert may be hot and wide, but life begins on the other side.'

Assuring you of our best endeavours at all times, we remain,

Yours faithfully,
Canaan Caravan Company

6

POTIPHAR'S WIFE

Genesis 39:6–21 tells the story of Joseph sold into slavery in Egypt and becoming responsible for his master's whole household. His integrity leads him through adversity to an eventual position of influence.

For further reflection or discussion

The adventures of Joseph are recounted with vivid detail and build a picture of the patriarch which begins when he is a rather obnoxious, know-it-all teenager and concludes at the pinnacle of his fame and influence as Chief Advisor to the Pharaoh. He is able in time of famine to help his own family and the whole of Egypt.

The land of Goshen (Genesis 47:6) was in the fertile eastern part of the Nile Delta. Contemporary Egyptian records show that it was government policy to allow famine victims from Palestine and the Sinai peninsula to occupy this area.

Captain Potiphar had entrusted Joseph with complete responsibility over his whole household, with the sole exception of his wife (39:9). Potiphar's wife (she is given no name) could have become one of the little people who change the course of history if Joseph had succumbed to her invitation.

The monologue takes a more sympathetic view of her, inviting us to glimpse another persona underneath the story. However, she does accuse him falsely and is responsible for his arrest and imprisonment. Although a slave, Joseph was not executed, as might be expected, 'because the Lord was with him' (39:23).

Suggestions for staging

An exotic tableau.

Potiphar's wife is very young and very beautiful. She is lying on a daybed while slaves fan her. She can be writing up, or reading from, her journal.

Egyptian costume consists of a twisted material headband, or a stiffened one with a cobra's head at the front. This can be worn over shoulder-length, straight, black hair which has a severe fringe (a wig is easiest!).

Slaves wear pleated, plain skirts tied with a sash that has one long and one short length. A white T-shirt is suitable, with upper arm rings and a circular overcollar made of coloured cloth or stiffened paper. This has a hole in the centre to drop over the head.

A noblewoman often wore a full-length overdress of light gauze with a pleated skirt below.

A WOMAN SCORNED

Dear Diary

Another day of flower arranging. Why can't the Nile flood early or something? Life is so boring. If only I'd known, I wouldn't have pushed Daddy so hard to get me married to Potiphar. But the Household Cavalry looked so good, so romantic. How was I to know? All he cares about are his horses and his drinking.

I do so miss everyone at home. The animals, the boats, the freedom. Is this what being a wife means? Spending half the day bathing and painting my eyelids and toenails. Laughing at old men's stupid jokes at dinner parties. Life was such fun at home. I remember the little things—the barbecues and the races; the word games; the shopping sprees; old fat Tutmor letting me make the soup; mother's sculpting.

What a fool I've been! Yet what other life could I have? Another girl to talk to would be good. She could tell me perhaps that this is our lot, what women are made for.

And now, deepest secret, there is the Hebrew. I cannot take my eyes off him, a slave. He smoulders and ignores me, and it's making him more fascinating. Don't misunderstand me, I love his looks and find him irresistible, but there is something more. He is a man who could be a partner. He is quick, skilful, intelligent, sensitive. He would be more than a lover.

I want him.

7
MOSES—SERVANT OF THE LORD

Exodus 2:1–15 describes the birth and early upbringing of Moses. 'There arose a new king over Egypt who did not know Joseph' (1:8). Moses' adoption by the royal family is identified as part of God's continuing purpose for the Hebrew people.

For further reflection or discussion

The name 'Moses' is a play upon both an Egyptian word that means 'to beget a child' and a Hebrew word meaning 'to draw out'.

The story of God's rescue of the infant Hebrew boy is one in which Pharaoh is unwittingly used through his family to bring up the very one who will deliver the Hebrews from captivity. Moses' sister Miriam (Numbers 26:59) is able to arrange for their mother to become his wet-nurse. When he is weaned, he is brought up as a member of Pharaoh's family.

Moses is a central figure in the history of Israel. He is a great leader who saves his people from slavery and acts as mediator in the covenant (binding contract) that God and his people make together at Sinai. Moses is perceived as a man of stature, of faith, of learning—a man who talks with the Pharaoh and with God face to face (Exodus 33:11).

Suggestions for staging

The setting is the Royal Schoolroom in the Court of Pharaoh Seti I.

The Royal Tutor should wear Egyptian costume. This could be much as suggested on page 27, although the tutor might wear a long ankle-length white robe with overcollar and headdress.

He is reading through a scroll to present to Pharaoh.

At the conclusion he indicates that he is satisfied and 'signs' it.

SCHOOL REPORT

Now, illustrious Seti, Great Pharaoh, I conclude my report of the Royal Schoolroom with a few observations about the Hebrew boy, Moses.

The Princess graciously adopted the boy and continued to take an interest in him until her sad death last year. He has (apart from the obvious cleanliness restrictions, necessarily imposed by our laws on all foreigners) been educated and treated in a comparable manner to the royal princes. His education in particular has equipped him for useful employment by Your Majesty, perhaps as a scribe or administrator.

That said, Beloved of Ma'at, the boy's head is stuffed with dreams and some residual nonsense to do with his people's tribal god. Where he got hold of the stuff, I cannot imagine. He has never been encouraged to have contact with his birth people. The abominable heresies of Your Majesty's unfortunate predecessor, Akhenaton, still survive, as you are aware, in some quarters. The notion of one god is a blasphemy that on Your Behalf cannot be tolerated.

Moses' abilities are enormous, his grasp of new and large ideas considerable. He has a natural charm and persuasive manner. With his favoured upbringing, he will make a useful leader of men. I feel that the time has come for him to be given some gainful task that will enable him to make his own way in the world. He cannot assume privileges without responsibilities. Nor must his sometimes wild notions be allowed to influence the young princes. My respectful suggestion, therefore, is that it is time for him to leave schooling and seek under Your Gracious direction, O Bull of Immense Strength, a means of repaying you and Egypt for all that he has been given.

I would simply add that the Hebrews seem to have become increasingly restless in recent times. Their usefulness, I know, is constantly balanced by Your Majesty against their potential threat as a foreign people within our borders. As if the Hittites were not enough danger! I know from our previous discussions that you believe Moses could be an ally in subduing his people. I have my doubts about that. Rather, I counsel, Great Pharaoh, that Moses be sent to one of your frontiers such as Nubia and the deep south where he can do nothing but good.

Esteemed Lord, Chosen of the Light, I Your servant,

Amon-guides-him
(Royal Tutor)

8

THE EXODUS

Exodus chapters 7 to 12 describe the plagues visited by God on Egypt because the Pharaoh would not release the Hebrew workforce from slavery. The story is one of courageous persistence on the part of Moses and Aaron and of disbelief on the part of Pharaoh and indeed of the people of Israel. Finally and reluctantly, after the devastation caused by the death of the firstborn males, Pharaoh lets the people go.

For further reflection or discussion

The exodus from Egypt occurred probably during the time of Pharaoh Rameses II in the thirteenth century BC. A group of refugee slaves sharing a common ancestry and religious beliefs moved from the Nile Delta region and settled in Canaan after a series of conquests.

Enough corroborative evidence is provided by archaeology to support this claim. For the Egyptians, it was probably a minor frontier incident, the loss of a large but replaceable group of workers building store cities.

For the Hebrews, it became a significant victory for their God and the moment when they knew themselves as a chosen people with a common identity and purpose. The Feast of Passover celebrated, ever after, God's wonderful redemptive acts. These began with the plagues of Egypt, many of them having natural explanations but providing the Hebrews with a cumulative demonstration of God coming to their rescue and bringing low the might of Pharaoh.

Lake Timsah is a marshy area which is an extension of the Gulf of Suez and the Red Sea and on the probable escape route.

Suggestions for staging

An outdoor setting with the character dressed in modern wet-weather gear and waterproof boots, perhaps as a nature reserve warden or someone similar.

The script is read in an educated but 'country' voice.

NILE WATCHERS' NATURE NOTES
SPRING NEWSLETTER

Dear Nature Lovers,

You don't need me to tell you that this has been an extraordinary and disastrous season. Whether you are a fisherman, market gardener, herdsman, fowl-snarer or just a plain lover of our native wetlands, you must feel as devastated as I do. A series of cataclysmic events has struck our beloved country and the Great River.

First it was the river running like blood. Fish, as you know, died by the tonne. It's been a terrible year for anglers, and lots of competitions have been cancelled. That was bad enough, but the freak conditions favoured frogs and these swarmed over the whole land. Usually a gardener's friends, the creatures have been uncharacteristically aggressive and very destructive. But the frogs could not destroy the hordes of gnats and flies that followed the stinking carcasses of fish. The natural cycle and intricate food chains have been disrupted and thousands of creatures have died. Many of you have sent in heartrending reports of whole colonies wiped out by disease.

Most recently, the dreadful storms of hail have threatened the crops, and famine is a real possibility throughout the country. What little standing grain there was has been further ravaged by the east wind bringing the dreaded locusts. Even more grim are the reports from all over the Two Kingdoms of the epidemic which has killed many male children. What have we done to so offend the gods? Never before have such awful conditions prevailed and now there is this strange darkness.

The land of Egypt is in desperate plight, Nile Watchers, and we are left reflecting what a delicate balance of life and nourishment is provided by our great river. Ra only knows what we can expect next.

And there is yet another strange phenomenon that several of our Lake Timsah readers have reported in the last few days. A kind of smoke column can be seen on the horizon. It cannot be more locusts, nor yet a wind storm, because at night it glows oddly. Let us hope this does not herald another disaster. We will be interested to hear others' views on what this mystery might be.

9
THE SCAPEGOAT

Leviticus 16:6–10 and 20–22 describe the ritual for the Day of Atonement. The notion that sin can be blamed on, or laid on, someone or something else is an ancient one but with plenty of modern resonances!

For further reflection or discussion

The ritual of the scapegoat is part of a tradition stretching back to the earliest days of the desert wanderings. On the Day of Atonement, two goats were chosen, one for the Lord and one for Azazel. The goat for the Lord was sacrificed to atone for the priests and people defiling the Holy Place because of their sinfulness. The live goat, the scapegoat, had the sins of the people 'laid upon' it and then was driven out of the camp into the wilderness. The Revised Standard Version of the Bible (followed here) names Azazel; other translations simply say 'wilderness' (v. 10).

The scapegoat is offered alive before the Lord 'to make atonement over it' (v. 10). Only then is it driven away. It is the God of the Hebrews alone who can forgive sins; the goat for Azazel, or the wilderness, is simply cast loose to wander, much as Cain was.

The conclusion is that the blood of the one goat cannot adequately expiate sin and the scapegoat is an attempt to evade responsibility for sin—to dump it somewhere far away. Azazel typifies this place that no one wants to know about or go to, the 'solitary land' (v. 22), and seems to be an evil spirit or desert demon.

An echo of such sacrifices and practices is found in the letter to the Hebrews, which speaks of Jesus suffering 'outside the gate' (13:12–13). His blood was spilt and our sins laid upon him.

Suggestions for staging

The character can wear token horns and a hair coat.

The monologue's tone progresses from a whoopee! feeling of freedom to growing anxiety in the final paragraph.

The name 'Azazel' is obviously crucial for prior or further comment or discussion (see above) and needs appropriate emphasis on the punchline.

TAKING THE BLAME

Freedom! Whew, I'm glad that's over. A very nasty moment back there. Sorry it had to be poor old Billy. We've known each other since kids and our nans made the crossing together. Still, what a way to go. Nice and clean; and for the Lord. If Billy had to die, this was a good, quick way.

I must say, they did him proud. Lovely service. The singing was good. The High Priest in his best robes. The works. And Billy—the poor fool. You could see him enjoying it all. He hadn't got a clue. Whereas me, I admit I was frantic. It took three of them to hold me. I really got the shakes badly. I got a glimpse of the knives and smelt the blood. No, I don't want to go through that again. And I won't have to.

Freedom! This is the life. Feed where I want. Travel at my own pace. Sleep or browse as the fancy takes me. This is much better than being with the herd. Here, I am me—an individual.

What a send-off! It seemed like everyone was patting me. Absolutely insistent that I was free to go. Positively pointing, almost driving me towards freedom. Out of the camp. Mmm! I can smell oregano. What a day! What a relief! What freedom!

Just one tiny little niggle from back there…
    They said I could go to Azazel.
    Is this it? Am I there?
    Or is it a person, a new owner?
    I don't fancy another owner.

Who or what is Azazel?

IO

BALAAM

Numbers 22 recounts the story of Balaam's ass. It describes part of the conquest of the promised land and demonstrates that Israel's God is the sovereign Lord of all nations.

For further reflection or discussion

The Israelites attempt to enter their promised land by way of Moab, east of the Dead Sea. King Balak of Moab summons Balaam, a Syrian diviner, to put a curse on Israel. Clearly he is worried by the threat of invasion but also by the growing reputation of Israel's God.

The well-known story of Balaam's talking ass has a touch of humour but makes a serious point. Balaam is a foreigner who heeds the voice of God and will do only what he is told (22:18); yet, great diviner that he is, it is only after his ass recognizes God's angel that he is obedient. Balaam then gets King Balak fussing around, building altars and making sacrifices, but still keeps him in suspense by refusing to come in person or curse the invaders.

In his discourses, Balaam makes it plain that his eyes are now well and truly opened (24:3–4) and Israel will be exalted—a massive morale boost to Israel.

It is not always the religious experts who are the first to see God in a situation. Often it is the simple and ordinary, even 'dumb' creatures.

Suggestions for staging

A tableau of an angel with drawn sword, and an ass with Balaam riding it could be devised. The ass should be on all fours and wear an open mask that does not impede speech. Balaam should sit on a covered upright chair placed behind the ass, as if riding.

Recorded noises of a braying donkey could be used at the start and finish.

DUMB CREATURE

This creature I permit to ride me
is a great diviner.
We live by the Euphrates river.
Many come to ask his sight or help.
But he could not see the Angel.

Humans are such dumb creatures,
crude and cruel, imperceptive,
obstinate, and full of self-importance.
Balaam is better than most.
But he could not see the Angel.

I do not wholly despair of one
who, though he beats me,
is at least open to the mind of God.
There are not many such
amongst the human kind.
But he could not see the Angel.

Sometimes when we are together,
or even when alone
and the humour takes us,
we asses bray our laughter
at these beings who think they are all-knowing,
in control.
It is fond laughter, tinged with regret
that such clowns cannot see the Angel.

11

ACHAN

Joshua chapters 6 and 7 tell the salutary story of Achan who disobeys God's instructions for the conduct of a holy war against the city of Jericho. The consequences of Achan's sin are swift, ruthless and (in context) necessary.

For further reflection or discussion

The ruthless treatment of Achan's family is compared with the way Rahab and her father's household are rescued (Joshua 6:22) by Joshua from the ruins of Jericho. Rahab betrays her own people, becoming a fifth columnist for Israel, and being honoured for it.

Achan, in common with all the people, knew that spoils from the sack of Jericho were 'devoted to the Lord' (6:18–19). His act was not simple theft, not merely blasphemy, but a breaking of the covenant (the special relationship) between God and his people (7:11).

At first, as this monologue suggests, the modern reader will be shocked by Achan's punishment, but it is possible that his story has contemporary significance. Tribal or familial guilt are not entirely foreign notions, even in our society. Who is to blame for forebears' mistakes or crimes? Who suffers the consequences? More particularly, can the present generation be held responsible for the morality it bequeaths to the next?

Suggestions for staging

A Bedouin tent forms the setting.

Achan (and members of his family) are dressed in traditional desert garb.

Achan unpacks his spoils as he speaks. The others react with delight (thereby associating themselves with his guilt).

The last phrase should be emphasized for the audience to absorb the unconscious irony.

STOLEN FROM GOD

Yes, my dears, I'm back safe and sound. I know you were worried, but God is good and we won! I've missed you too. What a day! You saw it all from the hills, didn't you? The city walls falling flat and the whole of Jericho ours. It was a walkover! Just one family saved, by order of Joshua—the family of Rahab who has helped Israel on the Lord's side. Remember her? The one who hid our expeditionary force. Everyone else, everything else, gone! That great city, greater than anything our oldest folk have seen in our wanderings.

But I have a surprise. My poor girls, I know how you feel it, not having proper dowries because I, son of Carmi, son of Zabdi, son of Zerah of the tribe of Judah, am the least of my father's household. I know how you, my good wife, strive to keep up appearances, to make ends meet, to hold up your head within our circle. That has changed. See, a rare and beautiful woven cloth for you, beloved, all the way from Babylon. And for my sweet twin daughters the price in gold and silver of a dowry each. We will bury it all here in this corner of the tent. It is our secret. God is indeed good. And will he deny us in our need? Have I not fought for him this day? I have saved from all of this great city such a very, very little. But for us it is a great deal—the difference, my dears, for us, between poverty and comfort, death and life.

I 2

SISERA

Judges 4 and 5. In the settlement of Canaan, God helps those who help themselves, and brings victory to the underdogs. The very elements fight on Israel's side in a brief but brutal campaign that brings peace for a generation.

For further reflection or discussion

The Song of Deborah (Judges 5) is generally agreed to be amongst the earliest portions of scripture. This is living history. One is almost on the battlefield of Megiddo, hearing the galloping of the horses' hoofs (v. 22), feeling the very heavens fighting on the Lord's side (vv. 4, 5, 20 and 21). Judges 4 is a prose account of the same event. Proper balance and full appreciation of the story requires reading both chapters.

By the time of Deborah, a prophetess who is judge (religious teacher and lawgiver), the Israelites have settled in the hill country of Canaan but failed to dislodge the Canaanites from the plains. Through the Valley of Jezreel ran the main highway from Mesopotamia to Egypt. Guarding the pass was the strategic fortress of Megiddo. It was to be the scene of many battles over the years (see, for instance, 2 Kings 23:29) and, according to religious tradition, will be the site of the final great battle. 'Armageddon' (Revelation 16:16) literally means 'hill of Megiddo'.

Sisera, commander-in-chief of the Canaanite forces, has nine hundred chariots of iron (Judges 4:3), constituting an enormous advantage. The Israelites did not as yet work with iron (Joshua 17:16–18). Barak, leader of the Israelite army, will confront Sisera only if Deborah goes with him (Judges 4:8). Deborah evolves a plan which is a re-run of the Egyptian debacle at the Red Sea (Exodus 14:24–25). She entices the chariots into swampland around the River Kishon where they are rendered useless. The weather, ordered by God (Judges 5:4), ensures the success of the strategy.

The victory song is a masterpiece of godly triumph and fearsome relish as it records Sisera's assassination. The poem ends with a cameo of Sisera's mother, an adroit comparison of his ignominious defeat and her overweening confidence. The assassin, Jael, is a fascinating character—a desert heroine of concentrated purpose. But the monologue chooses to concentrate on Sisera. What he regards as his strength, his unbeatable advantage, ends up destroying him.

Suggestions for staging

Sisera, in Second World War army fatigues, perhaps with a flak jacket and chewing a cigar, is haranguing his (imaginary) army before the battle. He is portrayed as a Hollywood soldier, a poseur, full of sound and fury…

OUTMANOEUVRED

Hear this, fellas! Gather round. A quick word before we move out. Now I know you've all been training hard for the last few months and this little show looks ideal to strut your stuff. Our ATVs should go through the enemy like a knife through butter. Momma ain't even gonna need to feel proud of ya. Treat it like another exercise. Enjoy.

Take a look, will ya, at those sad guys across the valley. Are they washed up, or are they washed up? They don't know what's about to hit them. You've got the best rolling stock going. We're talking state-of-the-art munitions. These All-Terrain Vehicles, I don't need to remind you, are iron. Tough, heavy, durable iron. To fight what? Bronze, that's what. To fight who? Barak, that's who. The mummy's boy. Has to do what the Holy Lady says. So whaddaya waiting for? Go get 'em. There's plunder a-plenty in that camp for all our womenfolk, or my name's not Sisera.

Just do the basics with these babes like I taught you and, above all, stick close!

OK. Mount up! Move out!

13
RUTH

The book of Ruth must be read in its entirety. It is very short and is the love story of Ruth and Boaz. It makes two points: love needs a helping hand, and love crosses boundaries.

For further reflection or discussion

The deeper message of the book of Ruth claims God for all peoples. Ruth the foreigner makes her own love and faith clear to her mother-in-law, Naomi.

'Where you go I will go, and where you lodge I will lodge; your people shall be my people, and your God my God' (Ruth 1:16).

Ruth is the epitome of a dutiful daughter. At Naomi's direction she risks even her virtue and is prepared to work humbly and diligently for them both.

Gentle Ruth is compared with shrewd Naomi who knows what needs to be done if they are both to have a comfortable life. Eventually the happy ending comes, but the punchline of the book is 4:17, which indicates that Ruth, a foreigner, was the great-grandmother of King David. It is her character and not her nationality that makes her pleasing to God.

Suggestions for staging

In this monologue, Ruth is a little livelier than she appears to be in the biblical story, opening up to her sister-in-law back in Moab in a natural way. She should be dressed in a full-length, woollen dress of quality, with a light shawl over her head, held by a circlet. She must appear as a 'nice' girl, modest but with a sense of humour. She is sitting on a stool, reading through the letter to be sent to Moab.

Dear Orpah,

I'm really, really sorry not to have written before. You must be wondering whatever has happened to us. Well, heaps. The big news is, I'm getting married!! So of course you must come. And stay if you want. I'm sure we can find you a handsome Hebrew.

But I'd better begin at the beginning... We got to Bethlehem safely, slap in the middle of harvesting. People were kind but pretty busy. Anyhow, we got a place to stay and then Naomi (looking back, I'm sure she had it all worked out) started networking. I went out gleaning. We hardly had two beans between us after the move, and anyhow I for one needed to demonstrate I wasn't a charity case. Naomi told me which farm to go to and it turned out to belong to Boaz. He's the one!! He's not old, but he's definitely mature. He's a distant cousin. And he's rich. But most of all, he's kind and lovely. As soon as he spoke to me out in the fields, I fancied him, and I know he came over specially to talk to me.

Hebrews have this arrangement where, if he wanted, as next of kin he could marry me. I didn't know that. Naomi did, though, didn't she! Trouble was, there was a closer relative. Ouch. He had a squint, bad breath and flat feet. Lucky for me he didn't push the claim. I rather think Boaz (who's quite rich, did I mention that?) bought him off.

So it's a love match! I'm so happy, Orpah. I hardly know how to deserve it. Naomi, bless her, will be set up for life, and we won't need to worry about her old age.

Do, do come. I promise you won't have to marry Squinty. I'm sending you the money for the fare. No problem. You can be the matron of honour. If you can't come, keep the money and buy yourself something wildly extravagant. But do write.

Your loving sister,
Ruth

P.S. You've *got* to come!!

14
SAMUEL

1 Samuel 3 describes the call by God of the young boy Samuel one night in the temple at Shiloh.

For further reflection or discussion

Luke may well have had the stories of Samuel's birth and boyhood in his mind as he began his Gospel account. Samuel's mother Hannah utters a song of praise (1 Samuel 2) which is echoed by Mary's Magnificat (Luke 1:46–55). According to Jewish tradition, Samuel was twelve years old when he began serving at the temple, the same age as Jesus when he talked with the doctors of the law at Jerusalem (Luke 2:40–52).

Shiloh was the central sanctuary at the time and had the privilege of guarding the ark of the covenant. The temple was served by Eli the priest and by his two worthless sons, Hophni and Phinehas (1 Samuel 2:12).

The story in Samuel is beautifully told. It is just before dawn. The lamp of God burns near the ark and the boy Samuel sleeps nearby. The awesome character of this most holy object, perhaps with the carved golden angels caught in the flickering lamplight, might have struck terror into any boy as he lay nearby (3:3).

It is a poignant moment in Israel's history—the worship of God in the care of one old man and a raw youth. 'The word of the Lord was rare in those days; there was no frequent vision' (3:1).

The message that the boy Samuel eventually receives from God begins with the splendid line:

'Behold, I am about to do a thing in Israel, at which the two ears of everyone that hears it will tingle' (3:11).

Samuel is portrayed in the story as a young innocent, loyal to Eli and faithful in God's service. The monologue is a reminder that he is also still a boy with normal feelings and reactions.

Suggestions for staging

Samuel should be played by a young teenager lying on the floor in a sleeping bag. A candlestick can stand nearby. He can wear a simple open-necked shirt and his script can be largely hidden in the folds of his bedding.

GOD CALLING

Hello, God. Are you there?
You're not there, are you?
Not when I need you.
Like when they gave me away.
I mean, think about it:
My own mother, giving me away.
How would you feel?
They can't love me.
I'm just a bribe.
A temple offering.
Nobody cares about me.
It's not fair!

If you were a real God
you'd thank me for giving up my life…
That iron chariot in the toyshop in Jericho, you'd give me that.
One measly iron chariot.
You could do that.
But oh no:
Samuel is dedicated to the Lord.
He doesn't want iron chariots.
He wants to do boring things in the temple.
Oh yes, I like being here in the dark on my own,
just that smelly old priest snoring.
Of course I do.
Smelly, smelly, smelly.
I don't see his own precious sons, Hophni and Phineas,
living in the temple.
No, I don't. Oh dear me, no.
Where are they? Out boozing, of course.
So why do I have to do this?
I don't even believe in you, God. So there.
Come on then, strike me down.
I dare you.
See, you can't.

It's so dark. I don't like it here.
I want my mum.
I want to go home!
This Ark spooks me.
I'm sure those gold angels moved...
I'm going to give them one more chance.
I'm going to look at them through my fingers.
There.
Help! Something is moving.
What's going on?
Please, God.
I do believe in you.
Stop it.
Really, honestly, truly, I do love you.
Just make it go away.

What was that? Someone called me.

Who's there? I can see you.
We can all see you, can't we?
And we're armed!!

There it is again! Someone calling,
Samuel, Samuel!
Oh, it's only old smelly Eli. What does he want now?

15
DAVID AND GOLIATH

1 Samuel 17:4–58 is a heroic story that demonstrates that God does not save by might, that he is on the side of the underdog.

For further reflection or discussion

Everyone knows the story of David and Goliath. The story of the little man with the guts and guile to volunteer for mission impossible. The story of Goliath of Gath the giant, champion of the Philistine army.

The reader is able to relish the detail of the story, the enormity of the odds, secure in the knowledge of the outcome, that the meek shall inherit the earth. Well, perhaps not the meek, exactly. The reader is invited to contemplate a young man who already has a firm grip on his destiny and the wit to turn weakness to his advantage. It was facing the military might of the Philistines, who had migrated from the north, that finally united the tribes of Israel. David, first as war leader and then as king, was to govern Israel for forty years, finally turning a tribal confederation into an empire.

Samuel played a pivotal role in bringing all this about as the recognized religious head of the tribes. The Bible narrative reflects his and others' ambivalence in promoting kingship: God is King; and yet his Kingship needs to be seen and felt in earthly terms (ch. 8).

Suggestions for staging

The monologue is from one of the Israelite conscripts with the kind of no-illusions rough humour of any soldier in any army.

A possible staging could include two or three soldiers in some kind of military uniform. They are gazing from a 'trench' over the top at the audience. The speaker comes on to join them at the start of the scene.

Never seen anything like it, mate. They told me he was coming out every day and making fools of us. Now I see it for myself. I've been running the family business whilst my brother did military service. Now we've swapped. But I'm wondering, what's the point? No one's going to get by that one. He's got to be three metres high. He scares the hell out of me and I'm not even thinking of fighting him. Look at that spear! It's like a weaver's beam. And the way he glitters. That poor little squaddie of a shield-bearer must sit up all night polishing that bronze. That's one batman's job I wouldn't relish.

So how long's he been coming out? Forty days? The stand-off can't last for ever. Saul's got no choice; we're going to have to fight. That's it, then. We're all dead.

You've got me doing it now. Everyone's like rabbits. We're scared stiff without him doing anything. I'd rather fight than listen to him laughing at us. Who's going to believe in God after this? Not that there will *be* an 'after this'.

Hang on. What's happening? Some fool is offering to fight over there. Oh, no... I don't believe it. It's some little squirt in a shepherd's skirt, not even armed. That is definitely it. They'll be so mad at the insult, we're all going to get massacred.

16
URIAH THE HITTITE

2 Samuel 11. The prophet Samuel's earlier reservations about kingship are confirmed. David behaves like a despot, taking both a wife and a life. This is a story of betrayed love: God's for David; and Uriah's for Bathsheba.

For further reflection or discussion

The background to this 'love letter' has all the ingredients of a block-buster novel—religion, sex, politics, betrayal. It is obviously a favourite tale and has a superb and distinct storyline from the wonderful opening lines: 'In the spring of the year, the time when kings go forth to battle...'

It is equally obvious that despite his sin and his crime, David manages to emerge as hero and winner. This was the typical behaviour of a contemporary ruler, and the king's repentance (see Psalm 51) must have seemed a rather decent thing to do.

Bathsheba, the eventual Queen Mother, might, just might, have engineered things somewhat. Who knows?

Uriah emerges from the story as the paragon of moral and patriotic rectitude. The following letter shows him as honest victim. In a story full of ironies, it piles on a few more.

Suggestions for staging

Uriah is in military costume, his helmet and sword laid aside.

He sits drinking wine at a small table with a lamp burning.

He reads the letter through in a gentle voice, full of emotion.

At the conclusion he blows out the lamp and lays his head down for sleep.

LOVE LETTER

Darling Bathsheba,

I am missing you terribly. I long to see your beautiful face and be back with you. It will be soon, I hope.

The war is going well and General Joab is an excellent commander, and yes, before you tease me, meeting even a Hittite's exacting military standards! The Ammonites are worthy opponents and have fought a good fight, but their city will fall and I shall return to hold you once again, most beloved.

I write this now to you in case you become concerned. Word will surely have reached you that I am at the king's palace. So near you, and yet so far! If I were to climb to the roof here I should see our lovely house and perhaps even gain a glimpse of you. But that is more than flesh and blood could stand.

Marrying you, fairest of Hebrews, I have cast my lot in with you and with my lord the king. Your people are now my people. Therefore I must hold to the vows that all we soldiers have taken... I shall stay ritually clean until the war is ended. Only then may I feast on your delights, O wondrous, wondrous wife. So I sleep the night here before returning with despatches for the General. But I can dream. And what better dream than of you, garden of all bounty? For your fragrance, your taste, touch and sight I ache and cry out in the night watches. This war has made me realize how strong my love is for you. May the Lord, God of the Hebrews, grant us soon a child to be my pride and your joy! That is more than my dream, dear one, it is my longing and my prayer.

You will be thrilled, Bathsheba, to learn that King David has been most kind to me and favoured me with many attentions. I am glad to have earned the king's regard. His concern even extends to you, sweet wife. He has asked many questions about you. Should you be fortunate enough to meet him in the coming days, I wish you to show him that we are among his most devoted and loyal subjects. Take any opportunity to repay his goodness to me. It is the duty we owe and may even lead to our further advancement.

To finish this letter is somehow to leave you, and that I cannot bear. You are ever in my thoughts. Know that, come what may, I love you always.

Your fortunate husband,
Uriah

17
JEZEBEL

2 Kings 9:30–37 demonstrates that God's opponents will eventually get their come-uppance, however attractive and successful they may appear.

For further reflection or discussion

The name Jezebel has passed into popular idiom as a description of a shameless, scheming, painted woman. She was a foreign princess with a lifelong devotion to the Baals, her people's gods. The name of her father Ethbaal as well as her own, Jeze-baal, emphasize this. Baal was the sky god of the Canaanites. Together with his three consorts, Anath, Ashtaroth and Asherah, Baal was invoked for rain and fertility.

Jezebel's story begins with her marriage to King Ahab of Israel (1 Kings 16:31) and continues through his long reign of twenty-two years with her strong opposition to God and his servant Elijah. In particular, her priests of Baal were defeated at Mount Carmel (1 Kings 18—20) and through her influence Naboth met his death on trumped-up charges so that his vineyard passed to the crown estates (1 Kings 21).

This, her final day, begins with her painting her eyes and adorning her head, thus identifying her as a foreigner with no regard for the more sober ways of Israel. Shameless hussy she might be, but her indomitable and spirited opposition to both Elijah and Elisha provokes our grudging admiration and has ensured that her name lives on. The script is an attempt to capture that spirit.

Suggestions for staging

It could be staged as if in a modern hairdresser's with stylist, manicurist, the works.

Jezebel can have her back to the audience but talk into the picture mirror in front of her.

JEZEBEL'S LAST MORNING

You see, darling, I'm supposed to be terribly wicked, but really I'm just your average queen. Not too much off over the ears, please, and I'll have the manicure now.

It's that man, that prophet—he spreads lies about me. First it was Elijah. Now it's the other one, Elisha. Troublemakers. Oh, and of course that po-faced Micaiah. He's a sly one. I'd like to wipe all their names off the fixtures list. Look at what they're doing now. Trying to make Jehu king. Do they think I don't know that's going on? Daddy always said, don't mix religion and politics. Keep the religious people sweet, he said, but keep them in their place. Trouble with these prophets is, they think their God's got some sort of monopoly. Then they go on as if they're in charge and not my son, Joram. They were a regular epidemic a few years ago and we sorted them. It's time for another prophet purging, don't you think? Once this war's over, Elisha is going to regret dabbling with Damascus and juggling with Jehu.

I'll have some of that dark henna, sweetie. And get a move on. Something's going to happen today. I feel it in my bones. Jehu won't attack Jezreel: nice, big, strong tower here. With a bit of luck and the help of Baal, we can surprise him and avenge Ahab, my husband. He was a good king, if a bit weak. That business over the vineyard. What was the fellow's name? Naboth. I ask you, darling, who's in charge here, king or prophet?

That's nice. Leave it like that. If Jehu, that Zimri, should come calling here at the House of Ivory, I think we can handle him.

Now, how do I look?
I feel drop dead gorgeous…

18

HARHAS

2 Kings 22:8—23:25 tells how the high priest, Hilkiah, finds the book of the Law in the temple during restoration work, and how King Josiah responds to God's word with a period of reformation.

For further reflection or discussion

This wonderful story is set in the time of the boy-king Josiah in the middle of the seventh century BC, a hundred years before the northern kingdom of Israel had been absorbed into the Assyrian empire.

In the southern kingdom of Judah, there is a time of uneasy peace as the distant borders of Egypt and Babylon begin to grow in power. The voices of the prophets Zephaniah and Jeremiah are heard in the streets of Jerusalem, but it is a woman, Huldah, who speaks out with the prophetic voice in this story.

The scroll which the high priest Hilkiah hands to secretary-of-state Shaphan is the book of Deuteronomy, long forgotten. The impact that it makes on young King Josiah is immediate and immense. In fear of the wrath of the Lord (22:13), he consults Huldah, who predicts that Josiah's penitence and humility will save him (22:19). Her grandfather-in-law Harhas (22:14) has lived through the long and wicked reign of Manasseh and is here depicted as a faithful soul delighted by the king's firm reforms.

Suggestions for staging

Harhas has been given the character of a modern Jewish tailor, perhaps working in the New York rag trade. It needs to be a monologue delivered with pace and polish.

Harhas is admiring of his granddaughter, and wise in the ways of court life.

Interjections are constantly thrown to members of his staff and the setting could therefore be a tailor's shop with bolts of cloth being unrolled and cut—a busy scene.

Harhas might be seated crosslegged on a high stool as he embroiders some small item.

THE KING'S NEW CLOTHES

So who would credit it, eh? Our little Huldah the prophetess consulted by the king. And am I proud? Harhas is very proud.

Kezia, girl! Careful with that cloth. Thirty camels fetch it from Susa and you throw it on the floor.

Aiyaah! You can't get good help these days. Still, things could improve now. The young king does his best. It's a good boy. All my life I wait for this moment. Frightened of Manasseh and his spies. Never daring to speak out against his nasty gods. Always hoping the old ways will return. Forty years the royal tailor, always watching what I say. Well, I have to, don't I? Or I swallow the pins.

Kezia, Joram. Look at what you're doing! My life, you'll ruin me, the way you cut cloth. Yish.

So what is it? The high priest finds a scroll in the temple he never knew he had. So they have so many they never get to read them? But now they read it and it's all news to the king—who is shattered, already. The secretary-of-state declares a national emergency. Emergency, schmergency. I smell a put-up job when it's waved in front of me. And our little Huldah? What does she say? God is angry, but maybe, just maybe, we get a reprieve.

That I should live to see this day! The word of God speaks again! All right, it's a judgment upon us. A poor schneider can live with that. And it's not all bad news. The king fears God's wrath. He repents in dust and ashes. So he tears his robes. So he needs new ones.

Kezia, girl, hand me the scissors!

19
SONG TO GOD

Psalm 139 celebrates that to be truly God is to know each person and thing in the most intimate and tiniest detail.

For further reflection or discussion

This is a simple paraphrase of one of the best-loved psalms. It speaks of a God who knows each one completely and who is even present (revolutionary idea, this) in Sheol. Sheol bears only a passing similarity to what Christians think of as 'hell'. Sheol is a place of shades, of the dead, where people retain only the faintest semblance of life. The psalmist emphasizes the precious and abiding relationship with God who is there for each person, no matter what.

The paraphrase omits an important aspect of the original psalm, which breaks into a lament to God about the wicked. If they are God's enemies, they are my enemies too, says the psalmist. It is possibly inexcusable to omit a portion of the psalm which does what many good psalms do— has a good moan (vv. 19–22). The present intention, however, is to emphasize God's intimate care and knowledge of each of us.

The psalms are full of such passion, of special pleading. They include a wide range of poetic and liturgical material collected over several hundred years. Although generally assigned to King David's authorship, it is clear that some of them date from the exile:

By the waters of Babylon, there we sat down and wept when we remembered Zion (Psalm 137:1).

There are psalms that curse God's enemies, psalms for special festivals, psalms of penitence, praise and petition. They are the imprint of a people's faith, containing passages that reach the heavens and yet others that remind the worshippers that they are fallible and flawed humans.

Suggestions for staging

This is a reflective prayer to be spoken perhaps out of a time of silence. It could be used as a reading at a funeral.

THE CHARTED SOUL

God, you have probed me to my innermost being.
You know what I am going to think, or say, or do.
And you always knew.
You reach out and touch me and I am yours.

There is no way I can remove myself from you.
In the depths of the sea you follow and find me,
in furthest space, or utter hell.
Nothing, even death, is dark enough to cover me.

Before I came to be, you knew me
and have watched over me from the womb
and down the years.
What you are and do is wonderful beyond belief.

I want my thoughts to be like your thoughts:
to hate what is negative, hurtful and evil.
All my life and beyond
I want to make you the way I should follow.

20

AMOS

Amos 7:10–17 provides some biographical detail of this austere prophet. His is the first voice of a different kind of holy person. He proclaims a message of righteous judgment. Prophets look into and beyond present situations to declare God's purpose.

For further reflection or discussion

Amos delivers an uncomfortable message in a time of national peace and prosperity during the long and stable rule of King Jeroboam II in Israel.

Amos came from the southern kingdom of Judah and was a village shepherd and a dresser of sycamore trees (v. 14). The trees were actually fig-mulberries which grew wild and needed little husbandry to produce a small fruit. As a down-to-earth countryman, Amos is particularly scathing about bland, ritualistic worship and the self-satisfied and complacent upper classes.

It seems likely that he was indeed expelled from Bethel, going home to his beloved country work. As the first of the written prophets, he or his disciples wrote much of his message down. It quickly became relevant and remains so as long as the dangers of institutionalized religion loom. Amos would have reacted strongly to words like privilege, preferment and precedence; or to religion seeming more interested in splendid buildings and ceremonies than in the plight of the poor or the urgency of repentance.

Suggestions for staging

Amos should be dressed as a shepherd of the period.

He enters carrying a bag of tools (crook, scythe and the like), which he puts down.

Raising his hands in prayer, he delivers the monologue in a rich brogue.

THE WILD TREE MAN

Well, Lord, you know I never wanted to come. You made me. Or at any rate, I felt driven. I'm a countryman. It's not my style, gallivanting about the royal shrine, judging my betters. There was nothing I wanted more than to be close to you, up there in the hills, a plain herdsman, and, oh yes, close to my trees. Plenty of air, plenty of time to think.

Maybe that's where I went wrong. I thought too much. Then I began to burn, to get angry on your behalf. What impudence, you must be thinking. I'm sure you laughed at me and my fig-mulberries, knowing I'd never get a decent crop from those old wild trees. And of course you were right. But they were there. I loved them. Part of my landscape, and free. And a challenge.

In a way, I suppose, Lord, those trees are a picture of my life. I wanted to cultivate them, get better crops. Just like I want to change these northerners back into a decent God-fearing people. What a fool I am, to think my little southern chapel ways were going to work at Bethel, your great and rich and ancient place.

The people here are snobs and hypocrites. All fancy titles and complicated laws to keep them rich and religious and everyone else poor and inadequate. They deserve anything you chuck at them, Lord—which I sincerely pray you will. And soon, because nobody believes me. Who listens to hard words in a soft season? So here I am before you, Lord, seeking to know what you want me to do next.

Amaziah has told me to push off home. They don't like me and my regional dialect. They don't like bumpkins claiming unpopular messages from God.

I don't want to be here. Shall I go home to Tekoa? Back to my trees and uncomfortable visions?

21

GOMER

Hosea 3:1–3 records the prophet buying back his adulterous wife because he loves her with the same steadfast love (6:6) that God has for Israel.

For further reflection or discussion

A very few years after the stern message of Amos (previous monologue), Hosea is preaching to the same people. The good times have gone and war looms. In the dozen or so years following the long reign of King Jeroboam II, four Israelite kings have been assassinated.

Hosea's message is not soft: he believes that Israel's rebellion deserves punishment by God (4:6) but, looking at his own marriage, he believes in eventual restoration (11:8). Gomer was probably a cult prostitute at one of the Canaanite shrines to Baal. Hosea marries her in good faith but she is unable to be faithful to him.

The prophet compares his own marital relationship with God's for Israel. God's redeeming love for his children means that he never gives up. Hosea also takes Gomer back time after time. Israel is constantly forgiven and wooed back, only to sin again.

During Hosea and Gomer's marriage, three children arrive, presumably not his. The children of her unfaithfulness are named Punishment, Not-Pitied and Not-My-People by the prophet. But the message does not get across, even though Israel's life, like Gomer's, is in turmoil. The country is in a state of anarchy and the Assyrian empire closing in for the kill. It is the more remarkable that Hosea can persist in a message of compassionate love.

Suggestions for staging

Gomer is over made-up and a bit past her prime. She wears modern clothes and carries a mobile phone. She is having a conversation with her lover but still trying for business. She moves about during the monologue and so positions herself so as to fade away off stage at its conclusion.

GOOD-TIME GIRL

(Over here, dearie! Fancy a good time?)

Take it, then, you pimp. That's all you think about—money. I don't
know why he does it—why he hurts himself. I'd like to think he
loves me at least as much as he loves that useless, rotten God of
his. When he took me, I thought he was fooling around. Another
religious gimmick. So I wasn't serious. I stayed on the game. And
I reckoned I was right when he gave the boy that weird name.

(Come on, love, you know you want to! Don't be shy.)

So things went on as always. Me having a good time. Not even
really cheating on him. Then you came along. You actually seemed
to care. I really do get it wrong, don't I? So I left him for you. He
still made the two girls his, even though we all know they're yours.
And I wondered. He never properly let go, did he? And you didn't
mind. Someone to pay the bills, making it easy.

(Like a mature lady, Sir? Clean and modest and biddable. Come
on, why don't you?)

He even got me feeling guilty. And, like I say, wondering. Now
this. And you aren't going to resist, are you? You're going to take
the silver, finish buying the house, and say 'Bye bye, Gomer.'

Suppose I can't blame you. Just a bit of hesitation might have been
nice. After all, it's been quite a while... So what happens next? I
pick up my stuff and move back in with him and the kids? Just like
that. And him. It's the second time he's bought me. Why? What's
his game? Perhaps he really does love me, the funny old thing, my
husband.

(Here you are, gents. Come and see old Gomer. She'll show you a
good time. It's experience that counts.)

22

DANIEL

Daniel 6 vividly describes how God looks after his own and is revealed as the living and universal God.

For further reflection or discussion

The concern of the book of Daniel is to demonstrate divine realities by telling six stories set in the time of the Babylonian exile. Four visions follow which offer predictions about the times soon to come when God's people will have ultimate victory in the midst of great powers struggling together.

Although Daniel has found favour and preferment under both Babylonian and Persian kings, he is still a true servant of God and will not compromise his faith. By a trick, his enemies inveigle King Darius into condemning Daniel to a night in the lions' den. His miraculous escape forces them all to recognize the sovereignty of Daniel's God.

Suggestions for staging

If the actor can convey the restless prowling, the roar and snarl and muzzling of these particular lions, it will make the monologue more convincing.

It need not be necessary to 'dress' the speaker but a mask could be worn.

THE LIONS' DEN

Most of the time it's not a bad life. It's not freedom, but we have this big courtyard and the paddock to roam in. Plenty of trees, shade and water. Usually lots to eat as well. Makes us lazy. We're predators really. This is all so easy. The food comes raw and ready.

Oh, we're in fine condition. Look at this coat and mane, glossy or what? It's usually better, but we've been starved the last three days. So we know there's a job on. We get to be locked in, and so hungry, it hurts. Everyone pacing up and down, lots of cat fights, stomachs growling. But the anticipation is good. We've been here before. Human flesh is hot and sweet and tender. The keepers always handle these times the same way.

Listen! Noises above. And are we ready! The grating overhead is lifted and all six of us are there, claws and fangs poised as the body is lowered. And something's wrong. We can't do it. Simply can't roar, slaver or tear. Something is stopping us, each one of us. We compare notes. One suddenly has a poisoned mouth, aching unbearably. Another can see a Shining One with a weapon guarding the body. No one attacks a Shining One. Another can't understand it, but just then he feels he can't manage another morsel. And me, I see Sheba in place of the body. Sheba, the mate they killed when they captured me far off in Kush. I can feel her breath, her warmth. I brush against her and we are cubs again. She fills my mind and, like the others, I forget I'm hungry.

How long this goes on, I don't know. Finally they lift the man out of the pit, alive and well. Immediately I could crush him but it is too late. The others have come to their senses as well, snarling, fighting, starving. What is happening? Is this some human form of torment? The grating stays off, so surely they're going to feed us. Hurry, hurry! Ah! Food at last.

23
JONAH

The book of Jonah illustrates that God cares deeply about all of humanity and the whole of creation.

For further reflection or discussion

The Bible is shot through with flashes of humour, such as Jesus' retort about husbands to the woman of Samaria (John 4) or the repetitive catalogue of musical instruments in Daniel 3.

But the book of Jonah has a delightful if pointed humour throughout. The whale and the worm are particularly memorable. The notion of Jonah spending three days inside a great fish with the attendant smells and frights is great fun. And the book ends on an ingenious bathetic note about the silly, simple people of the city 'who do not know their right hand from their left, and also much cattle'.

The joke for this script is to look at how the other 'victim' feels. Whales, those gentle giants of the vast reaches of the ocean, suggest a divine innocence. Neither this whale nor Balaam's ass can seriously believe that humans have souls. How could they? The whale instinctively knows that they have moved away from God to the point of having no knowledge of or relationship with him. Yet the purpose of the book of Jonah is to remind everyone of the wideness of God's mercy and how his love is for everyone. This is a story to introduce a God who is not a narrow nationalist deity but a universal redeemer.

Suggestions for staging

Deep ocean sounds or pictures including whalesong could introduce and accompany the delivery of this monologue.

It would be best done by a hidden actor whose voice is well amplified and given an 'echo'.

OUT OF THE DEEP

Hello, mother!

Thank you for the notes and vibes which just arrived. It's good to know you and the Old School are doing well.

Just thought I'd make waves towards you for a while as something rather out of the ordinary happened to me a couple of days ago. The Great One sent a message for me to swallow a land creature. Ugh, do they taste horrible! Not that I chewed it; I had to swallow it whole. It's here now, moving about, making me quite bilious.

Goodness knows (well, of course It does) why me and what for. These things are not particularly pleasant to taste or in any other way. I know you warned me. These puny creatures, riding on flotsam, loving to hunt our kind if they can without trouble! They are smelly, dangerous, useless. Worst of all, they have no soul. How could they, and for what? And yet, why does the Great One want it?

The strange thing is, I have felt it trying to send signals to the Great One. When all is said and done, in the infinite purpose of the ocean, can this tiny pain have meaning?

Mother, did this ever happen to you?

Keep smiling.

Your loving
Leviathan

24
ZECHARIAH

Luke 1:5–23 is the real starting point of Luke's Gospel. A precise point in history is given and the story of the miraculous birth of John the Baptist, latter day prophet and herald of the Kingdom, is told in a way which immediately grips and informs the reader. The voice of prophecy has been silent for four hundred years. Now a new order is beginning, superseding the old.

For further reflection or discussion

Temple sacrifices at the time of Jesus were carefully ordered events day by day. The whole country was divided into twenty-four divisions of priests and Levites who took a week's turn at offering a lamb and the incense. More elaborate ceremonies occurred on the Sabbath and at great festival times.

For an ordinary priest like Zechariah of the division of Abijah, the opportunity to be at the centre of temple ritual was regarded as the ulti-mate honour and joy.

The temple was controlled by the party of the Sadducees who stuck strictly to tradition and came largely from an aristocratic background. The Sadducees had no belief in resurrection or in angels.

Even Zechariah, who probably wasn't a Sadducee, has to be prompted by the archangel's splendid and searing words:

'I am Gabriel, who stands in the presence of God; and I was sent to speak to you, and to bring you this good news' (v. 19).

Of course, it is news that Zechariah is forced to keep to himself as he is struck dumb.

Suggestions for staging

This monologue pokes gentle fun at the pomposity and preciousness of some contemporary hierarchies and traditions by using the setting of an

English cathedral and making its Dean the high priest. Digging more deeply, it suggests that the religious institution can obscure rather than reveal God.

In staging it, the Dean, probably in full robes, should sweep in and sit behind a very large desk, addressing a small shadowy figure with its back towards the audience.

BY APPOINTMENT

Well now, Mr Zechariah, I've asked you back here to the cathedral for a debriefing. This is all most unfortunate and a touch embarrassing.

I will be plain. You were invited here in good faith when it was your turn as a country preacher to lead the worship. A very, very great privilege, I'm sure you appreciate. You must be aware that we have a strong contingent of very able priests, many with specialist ministries and with considerable learning and ability, attached to this cathedral foundation. Any one of them is more than capable of a very satisfactory, not to say compact, sermon to order. But we have this policy of involving you good folk from outside the city. We like to include you now and then, give you a part to play. Quite so. And that is why you were here as Duty Chaplain last Wednesday and leading Evensong.

Now I am afraid that I as Dean have received a number of complaints about you. I much regret having to say this, but I am a firm believer in getting these things out in the open. It may help your future ministry if certain things are explained to you, even though I have to tell you that, sadly, you will not be receiving any further invitation from us. As I say, this is all rather embarrassing. You are a priest old enough to be my father. But there it is.

And really, really, we simply cannot allow our worship to become so protracted. The choir were quite indignant at the length of the service. Whatever kept you so long? We pride ourselves on keeping strictly within the boundaries of one hour.

I must add that you appear to have crossed other boundaries, and this has offended several important and influential members of our congregation. We are not accustomed here, Mr Zechariah, to religious ecstasies or visions. There is no place for them in our cathedral worship. As an important element of the Establishment, we seek to preserve at all times a proper dignity and decorum.

Nor, I must emphasize, are visions of angels something that we countenance in divine worship. If it had been one of these younger priests with their somewhat different and exuberant style, I might have understood although not condoned it. But from *you*! We have no relish for the charismatic or blatantly low church. Angels are not the way we do things here in the cathedral, Mr Zechariah.

You will gather from what I have said that there will not, cannot, be a repeat of this inappropriate kind of worship. But I want to be fair. Have you anything you wish to say? Anything at all you can offer in mitigation or explanation?

Speak up, man!

25
CHRISTMAS

Luke 2:7 is one tiny reference that completely captures the manner of the incarnation. God couldn't have been better 'earthed' than this!

For further reflection or discussion

Bethlehem was obviously a complete shambles that first Christmas Eve, as Joseph found to his cost. Poll tax payers were flocking in to register, or possibly meeting in secret to oppose it and joining a reformed Zealot Party.

The sense of chaos and confusion in the little town is expressed in this monologue.

Unrelenting bureaucracy is always a feature of occupied countries. The unfortunate innkeeper, having probably made a small fortune over the census period, is to be forced to close.

Suggestions for staging

Somehow, red tape is more believable than tinsel.

This monologue might be performed by a very proper female civil servant, smart outfit, flashy spectacles, laptop much in evidence, and with an officious manner.

She could end by slapping a red 'CLOSED' sticker on the door of the inn.

DEPARTMENT OF HEALTH,
PROVINCE OF JUDEA

Dear Sir,

A recent inspection of your property known as 'The Key of David' Public House, situated in the town of Bethlehem within this province, found you in breach of government regulations.

On the night of December 24th, your inn, with licensed accommodation available for a maximum of thirty persons, had approximately seventy-six people sleeping on the premises. Our Inspector was told that forty-six of these individuals were members of your family. However, the recently completed census clearly shows that your family consists of five people.

Whilst visiting the town, our Inspector received a quantity of complaints from your immediate neighbours of music played at an unacceptable volume for a built-up area. As one informant put it, the music 'seemed to fill the whole sky'. May we remind you that your licence does not extend to music and dancing.

You are further accused of exceeding the prescribed licensing hours for serving intoxicating beverages. As you are no doubt aware, summonses have been issued for out-of-hours drinking to a number of your patrons, including several shepherds employed by the municipality to watch over their flocks by night.

However, this notification is chiefly concerned with the fact that our Inspector found a newborn baby in a part of the inn reserved for domestic animals. Apart from the obvious disregard for basic hygiene, further investigation adduced the information that no midwife attended the birth, that the parents were itinerants, and that the said stable or cowshed was visited by foreign people without valid immunization certificates.

It is our duty to warn you that we shall be applying for a closure notice on your business and that a substantial fine will be levied for the above breaches of health and safety regulations.

Yours faithfully...

26

THE MURDER OF THE INNOCENTS

Matthew 2:16–18 gives a sense of urgency and horror to the narrative. The King whose Kingdom is not of this world (John 18:36) is none the less sought by the Magi as an earthly king and Herod's subsequent action is decisive and politically motivated.

For further reflection or discussion

In the story of the murder of the innocents there are echoes of an earlier story. The book of Exodus (1:15–22) records the instruction of Pharaoh to his people to drown all male Hebrew babies. Moses was saved, as was Jesus in this account, for a work of redemption. Matthew quotes the prophet Hosea (11:1): 'Out of Egypt have I called my son!' It is from exile in Egypt that the child Jesus is restored to the promised land.

King Herod ruled from Jerusalem from 37 to 4BC. His rise to power had been fraught with hazards. He consistently backed the wrong Roman leaders, just as his father Antipater had done. Yet he always managed to extricate himself from each new threat to his political survival. Although Herod's family was Idumaean (Edomite) and he was looked upon as a usurper and a client-king of Rome, he achieved a great deal during the thirty-three years of his rule. He improved the internal economy, built new cities and rebuilt the temple in Jerusalem.

At the time of the birth of Jesus, Herod's rule was drawing to a close. He was faced with a series of dynastic intrigues and murders within his family. (He had married ten wives and had fourteen children.) Jesus was no threat to Herod's earthly power. Still less were those caught up in the massacre. So often, it is innocents who suffer. The Bethlehem babies are a reminder of all victims of the dark and violent side of humankind.

This monologue presumes to capture something of the devastation that mothers must feel when their babies die or are killed. It must be a hopeless love that leaves them torn and empty. Because of who Jesus was and what his life was saved to do, the final paragraph hints at the unconquerable love of Easter that turns a dead end into a new beginning.

Suggestions for staging

If an actor is used, this monologue requires sensitive treatment and is best done without props or frills.

A woman's voice, quiet and controlled, will allow the words to speak. Gentle background music might be appropriate.

INNOCENT

Hello, baby. The sun is bright today, the birds are singing, just like the day you were born.

Everything seemed super-real then. Holding you, flesh of my flesh, close. Loving the smell of you, the funny, important, small noises you made.

Having you made me complete. Loving you made us a family, tripled our love. I miss you. I miss that you cannot talk back, cannot grow up.

Coming here, I am near you. I will always come. I will try to talk, but mostly I want to squash you close, as I did when you were snatched away.

And I cannot.

See, my tears fall like stars on your little, little grave and turn into flowers. My grief is not anger, only longing. If I could know that love, one day, will allow me to reach through death and touch you!

Rest for now, my baby.

27
THE WISE MAN

Matthew 2:1–12 is the only account of the wise men's journey to find the Messiah. They represent the discerning world and bring appropriate gifts.

For further reflection or discussion

We do not know how many Magi journeyed to Bethlehem, nor that they were kings. That said, the wise men begin to give the incarnation a universal significance. As representatives of the East, they mingle with other Gentiles at the court of Herod the Great in Jerusalem, place of the temple but also a crossroads of culture, religion and civilization.

The Church quickly recognized that, through the Magi, the Christ-child had been shown to the nations. And for early Christians and for Eastern Christians today, the feast of the Epiphany is more important than Christ's birthday. Epiphany means 'showing' and celebrates that the Christ-child is shown to the whole world. The perception of the Magi is first, that Christ is born, and second, that he is born for all.

Magi came from the region of Persia and formed a learned class. It would appear that these particular Magi were not wise enough to realize that announcing a rival claimant to the throne was a maladroit approach to Herod. Hence this picture of a wise man who has to be 'managed' by his wife.

We of course know that the wise men got it right, but Lucia is there to remind us that none of the obvious signs suggested they had.

Suggestions for staging

Lucia, dressed in many jewels and shawls, can be reading through her letter to Caspar. As she does so, she can (if desired) be handing out other copies to a succession of servants who depart hastily in different directions to 'trace' Caspar.

CASPAR

CASPAR, you wretched man, you exasperating husband!

Ignore my previous letter. And in case this grossly overrated Roman postal service has failed yet again, I wrote to say come home at once. You have been a year or more on this lunatic quest and enough is enough. Heavens know I see little purpose or profit in this magi business but at least here, under my eye, you can get on with your work and charge proper rates. A pity the stars didn't tell you how long and how futile this journey would prove!

But to my point. I have just received your letter postmarked Bethlehem (wherever that is) and have read it with increasing and incredulous horror. As I understand it, you claim to have found some sort of royal child basking in the light of this famous star of yours. Said child was apparently the son of a carpenter living in rented accommodation in some third-rate provincial town. You have further presented the child with the gold you took, which I for one saw as an investment on some future appointment as Astrologer Royal. Have you taken complete leave of your senses?

Get back to this Bethlehem place and recover the gold or answer to me. I am sending copies of this letter to all the likely staging-posts on your journey. What your erstwhile companions make of all this, I cannot imagine. They can't possibly have supported your wild claims or action. Call yourself a wise man? Get that gold and get back here at once!!

Your ever loving wife,
Lucia

28

MARY

Luke 2:41–52 is the story of the boy Jesus talking in the temple at Jerusalem with doctors of the law. This biographical fragment is intriguing mostly because it is all we are told of the 'lost years' of Jesus, but also because Luke describes a pre-teenager, single-minded and heedless of others' feelings, in search of his vocation.

For further reflection or discussion

The Gospel stories are written by the four evangelists out of their own and the Christian community's faith years after the resurrection. But there can be little reasonable doubt that they recall and explore an authentic story. Jesus of Nazareth's sayings and doings are remembered with intense and loving fervour. The gospel is not make-believe. More serious attempts would have been made to erase discrepancies and give uniformity to the gospel story if it were.

Reading the gospels is to discover that there are times when the words and acts of Jesus are faithfully set down even when their significance was not apparent to the recorders. Equally, and because never in any age is history a mere list of facts and dates, the Gospels are written in faith to interpret faith.

In this present story, some may want to find an implicit religious message. Jesus' response to his parents (v. 49) certainly suggests one. It is a recognition and acceptance of his vocation similar to those of the old prophets.

But this story is also and more obviously a warm human one. What mother has not been through a whole range of emotions when her teenage son or daughter stops out? What teenager does not have his or her own agenda and impatience with parents?

The Mary of this monologue typifies such a mother. She has feelings and she expresses them. The passion of the Magnificat (Luke 1:46–55) or the loving confidence as she instructs the wedding servants (John 2:5) suggests a woman who knows her own strengths. Perhaps she is recognizing in this moment the pain of letting go as the adolescent begins to find his own way—the shadow of the sword that is to pierce through her own soul (Luke 2:35).

Suggestions for staging

Mary can be accompanied by Jesus. They should be dressed in traditional robes. The monologue could begin at the back of the church (if performed there) and the actors only move gradually into view as they leave the temple.

MORTIFIED

That was so embarrassing! Whatever can these priests imagine we are doing as parents? Allowing you to roam off for two whole nights. Presumably thinking we couldn't care less about you? That we'd blithely go off back to Galilee without bothering to check if you were in the caravan? I mean, of course we thought you were. Same as on the way down. Half the time you weren't eating or travelling with us. You *knew* what time we were leaving. You must have known we'd be frantic. How could you do this to us, Jesus?

Please hurry. I just want to get right out of the temple, right away from Jerusalem. Your father's not as young as he was. He's been in agonies these last two days. You know how seriously he takes his responsibilities.

I realize how badly you wanted to come to Jerusalem. You've been talking about it all year. But cities are trouble. Jerusalem is a dangerous as well as an exciting place. And you haven't made things easy. I know you mean well, son, and I know you're sincere, but just think. Back there you were pushing the questions. It could easily look to be too clever by half. These doctors of the Law don't like being outsmarted.

You're twelve. I know that means you think you're grown up, supposed to be responsible. But you're still our little boy. We love you. I'd hate to lose you. I've been sick with worry. Promise me, darling, you won't do anything like this again.

29
JOHN THE BAPTIST

Matthew 3:1–12 describes the appearance of John the Baptist in the wilderness by the River Jordan. John's message was for God's people to return (repent) from spiritual exile and become a new people of God, washed and ready for the coming Lord (v. 11). Everyone can hear and respond to this message.

For further reflection or discussion

John the Baptist was recognized as an old-style prophet. He preached judgment and repentance and a practical concern for one's neighbours. Some of his ideas were influenced by contemporary religious groups such as the Essenes and the Pharisees. Such groups were particularly concerned with rites of purity through washing. The acted parable of baptism—immersion in water for the cleansing of sin—will for ever be associated with John's name and ministry.

Jesus' own baptism of followers will be 'with the Holy Spirit and fire' (v. 11), a distinction that emphasizes that John's baptism is preparatory and that of Jesus is conclusive and complete.

The Christian rite of baptism owes much to Paul:

Do you not know that all of us who have been baptized into Christ Jesus were baptized into his death? We were buried therefore with him by baptism into death, so that as Christ was raised from the dead by the glory of the Father, we too might walk in newness of life (Romans 6:3–4).

Like the prophets of old, John was singled out by God and came to an understanding of his role and message through a tough discipleship. His circle of influence included disciples (Luke 7:18–23), and a wider knowledge of his teaching endured beyond his death and that of Jesus (Acts 18:25; 19:1–7). John preached the coming of the Kingdom and always saw his role as subsidiary to that of Jesus.

The greatest prophets and their message have often been suffocated by religious hangers-on, there with transient fervour for a temporary sensation. Our picnickers are supposed to typify such people but Auntie produces a surprise and 'walks forward for baptism'.

Suggestions for staging

Two actors come on in traditional robes. They sit on a low bench with their backs to the audience.

The character of Auntie does not speak but anticipates the script with the required movements: attempting to share her coat, standing up, and finally walking forward and off stage.

Auntie may be rather deaf but she hears God's call all right.

The speaking character, solicitous but a little patronizing, is finally left to chase after Auntie, still shouting.

Sit down here, Auntie. This looks a nice dry spot. And we should get a good view of the prophet from here. My, what a lot of people. They said there would be, but I never expected this many, did you?

I SAID, I NEVER EXPECTED TO SEE SUCH A CROWD. NO.

Shall we start on the picnic? I'm famished. Your poor feet must be killing you. Perhaps we can have a bit of a paddle afterwards.

A BIT OF A PADDLE. YES.

Cheese or chicken?

Well, I must say, he's got a nice day for it. I'm ever so glad we came. You all right, Auntie?

I SAID, YOU ALL RIGHT, AUNTIE? GOOD.

Look! Something's happening. It's him! Oh dear. Bit scruffy, isn't he? Still, I suppose you expect that from a prophet. Not like priests, are they? All lah-di-dah and ever-so-clean robes.

He's going to talk. Can you hear all right, Auntie?

No, dear. BROOD OF VIPERS.

Lovely, isn't it? He does talk lovely. Real passion. Wrath and stuff.

I SAID, WRATH.

Quite worked up, isn't he? I like the bit about hellfire.

No, Auntie, I don't want your coat. You can share it afterwards, if you must.

Any more cheese?

Sit down, Auntie. You don't have to go. It's just the ones that want to wash and start again. No, I don't think so. We came for the talk, didn't we, dear? And you'd catch your death.

I SAID, CATCH YOUR DEATH.

Stay here. You can put something in the collection.

COLLECTION, AUNTIE. WHEN IT COMES ROUND.

Well, that was *very* interesting, wasn't it, Auntie? A real treat to hear.

I'll just pack our bits and pieces away. If you're ready, Auntie, it's a fair old walk home.

Not that way, Auntie.

Auntie! Where are you going?

Stop! We only came to watch.

COME BACK, AUNTIE!

30
ZEBEDEE

Matthew 4:21 and 20:20 provide two glimpses of the Zebedee family. Blessed are those who leave everything for the sake of Christ and the Kingdom. But there is also a cost to those they leave behind.

For further reflection or discussion

Capernaum is on the west bank of the Lake of Galilee, near the top. To the north is snowcapped Mount Hermon. To the south, the ground rises steeply to where Nazareth lies on a high and windy moorland. The Jordan Valley offers fierce and burning heat in the summer, the lake itself being 682 feet below sea level.

Climatic contrasts such as these mean that a sudden storm can spring up almost from nowhere to endanger fishing craft on the lake. It made sense for fishermen to form small fleets in partnership.

In Zebedee's time, the fish were plentiful. Boats from the towns of Magdala and Tiberias as well as from Bethsaida and the Ten Towns on the eastern shore competed for trade. The wooden boats were small, with oars and a single sail. Zebedee's enterprise was big enough to employ hired servants and to provide a living for himself, them, and his two sons James and John.

Suggestions for staging

Zebedee is dressed in fisherman's clothes, either ancient or modern.

He is repairing a net on an upturned lobster pot.

He is calling after his departing (invisible) sons, making his points in a crescendo of emotional blackmail and self-pity.

NET WORK

Don't do this to me. I've spent my life building up this business. Zebedee and Sons. Look at us. The biggest boat on the lake, four hired servants, and Capernaum's best fish restaurant. How am I supposed to manage without my sons?

A lovely little enterprise we've got going here. I've been proud of the way you've worked things up with me. Did I ever tell you that? Your old dad could go any time. I'd die happy to pass things on to you. Not as young as I used to be and the arthritis hits me something cruel on these night trips.

But no matter. You shove off, the pair of you. Go on, we'll cope somehow. Probably better than you, I reckon.

Who pays your precious preacher, eh? How's he going to keep and feed four grown men, eh? And how long before he's yesterday's religious crank, eh? Right fools he's making of you lads. I did think Simon had more sense—him with a wife *and* a mother-in-law to worry about. Who's taking over their boat, I'd like to know?

Go on, then. Leave all that. We'll pick the nets up. We'll get them mended somehow before tonight's fishing.

That I should live to see the day! Both my sons leaving me. After all I've done for you. And what your mother's going to say, I dread to think. It'll break her heart. She had such plans for you. So proud she is of both of you. Now you're chucking your lives away.

What can this Jesus give you? Money, crowns, a place in heaven? Don't make me laugh.

3I
JOHN AND HEROD

Mark 6:17–29 describes how John the Baptist's uncompromising message leads to his death. He is last in the line of persecuted prophets and first in line for 'Christian' martyrdom.

For further reflection or discussion

Herod Antipas had assumed power in Galilee upon the death of his father Herod the Great. He was to rule as Tetrarch until his death in AD39. Thus his reign coincided with the whole life of Jesus.

Herod's love for Herodias defied both Roman foreign policy and Jewish religious law. He was already married to a princess of the Nabataeans, a country that formed a buffer state on the eastern frontier of the empire. Herodias in her turn was already married to Philip, Tetrarch of Ituraea and Herod's half-brother. For the latter reason, John the Baptist denounced Herod and was imprisoned.

It is unlikely that strict Jews would go anywhere near the foreign, tainted city of Tiberias, built by Herod Antipas to flatter his Roman overlords. But plenty of people, as in every time and place, would enjoy celebrities, especially royal celebrities.

Suggestions for staging

This monologue is written as if for an outside television broadcast.

It should be staged in modern dress and the reporter can stand in front of a 'camera crew' with cardboard camera, broom used as sound boom, etc.

HEROD'S BIRTHDAY

Hi! You're tuned to Gaza Strip TV. This is Simeon Rumah, your Special Court Correspondent and Royal Watcher Extraordinaire.

Everyone who's anyone is here in Tiberias today for Herod's birthday celebrations. Even Pontius Pilate, the Procurator, tells me he has a small but valuable packet to deliver from the Emperor. And we all know that no love is lost between PP and Herod Antipas.

Party guests are arriving constantly in readiness for tonight's big palace thrash. Probably the only person in the palace not out for a good time is religious freak, John the Baptizer. The party pooper will still be cooling his heels in the dungeon after insulting the new royal family.

Flags are flying and the crowds have been gathering since first light. Any excuse to start drinking and stop working... A short time ago their patience was rewarded as the royal entourage swept in from Caesarea. The Lady Herodias, newly married, is still exciting plenty of interest—a stunningly well-made-up lady with a heap of allure and dressed in the latest Roman mode. She's all set to be style guru on the mega scene of Palestine.

But even Herodias is outglammed by daughter Salome. The princess has just returned from Athenian finishing school and wow! is she stunning. Hers is a wildly exciting beauty that makes strong men throw their javelins an extra ten paces and charioteers drive straight into walls.

Herod as both uncle and stepfather seems keen to get Princess Salome established in court circles. Things kick off tonight with a rather special birthday celebration, we understand. Word is that the princess does an amazing dance. Just her, some music, seven veils and three beads. Those who've seen her practise say the effect is devastating. By royal command, Salome will dance tonight. Women will be mad with jealousy and men will lose their heads. Watch this space for a full report tomorrow.

This is Simeon Rumah for Gaza Strip TV, outside the palace, returning you to the studio.

32
JESUS AT CANA

John 2:1–10 is the story of the wedding feast at Cana, a mere half dozen miles north of Jesus' home village of Nazareth. For John, a 'sign' is as much acted parable as miracle. What is delightful is the ordinary, happy context of the sign—a village wedding. The extraordinary is found in the commonplace.

For further reflection or discussion

Turning water into wine at a wedding reception seems somewhat frivolous for Jesus' first sign. The context in John's Gospel is important: the water jars are for purification and are filled with something new and good.

Jesus moves on immediately to Jerusalem and cleanses the temple (2:13–16). He then holds a dialogue with a Jewish leader called Nicodemus about being 'born anew' (3:3). Next, John the Baptist is talking about purifying (3:25) and Jesus speaks to the Samaritan woman about himself as the wellspring of eternal life (4:14).

In such ways the teaching moves on and there is little doubt that the wedding wine could foreshadow those with a new faith transformed at the heavenly banquet yet to come.

The bride's snobbish mother-in-law makes the main point again: there is a superabundance of best quality wine. God's generosity knows no bounds!

Suggestions for staging

This monologue could be set up with two ladies at a café table with carafe and glasses.

The listener does nothing but nod her head, purse her lips, hold out her glass…

MORE WINE?

I have never been so mortified in all my life. But I should have known. The whole thing was always going to be a farce and, to my mind, a disaster. My son, a farmer of substance; our family, with its lands and ancient name. And that girl. No social graces. The family, complete nobodies. The father is a potter or tinker or somesuch. It was a mismatch from the first. The least the fellow could have done was to accept our help with the wine list and spared us some embarrassment. But no. 'I'm the bride's father: it's my job.' So we leave it. Reluctantly, we leave it.

And what happens? Well, you were there, dear. That wine was frightful, wasn't it? Heaven knows where he got it. What I say is, thank goodness they did run out. I don't mind telling you, it was a terrific effort to keep smiling while drinking the stuff.

Now, you know I've got no time for this Jesus person. I couldn't believe that they had invited him, his hedge priests, and the whole darn family. I ask you! But I have to admit he came through with the goods. How he did it I don't know but it was graciously done, and a magnificent present. Hiding that immense amount of quality wine in the washing jars took a bit of organizing.

I have to hand it to him. Don't like him. Carpenter, isn't he? But not the quack I first thought.

Have another glassful, dear. We've got stacks to get through...

33
JOANNA, WIFE OF CHUZA

Luke 8:1–3 describes something of the social and religious revolution Jesus was initiating. Here he makes women visible among his disciples.

For further reflection or discussion

Tiberias, chosen and developed by Herod Antipas as his capital and modelled on Roman urban design, grew to be an important centre of influence and communication for the whole Judean province. Well-paved roads led to it and the major trade routes from Egypt to Damascus, which since ancient times had passed close by, were linked to it.

Jesus' Galilean ministry would have been conducted not merely to north-country farmers and fishermen but to a rich variety of people. Those who settled in the new town came often from a sophisticated or 'Greek' background that made them unacceptable to the more conservative Jews. Still more shocking, Jesus included women in his teaching and company! His words filled them with amazed excitement in a way that was not to happen in more traditional places.

Joanna, as wife of an important palace official (he is particularly identified in the story), would not settle for a menial task unless she chose to. Elsewhere Jesus demonstrates his own willingness to be servant (John 13:5 etc).

Suggestions for staging

Joanna can be composing the letter to Chuza. She should move around, pacing her delivery, making corrections, musing. She appears as self-assured, not blatantly feminist, but a sensible, mature woman of the world.

A FIRST FOR WOMEN

Chuza, greetings!

I said I'd let you know how we were getting on. We're still buzzing around the lakeside and the response to Jesus is phenomenal!

My dear, you made yourself an outsider when you agreed to be Herod's steward and, of course, living in Tiberias has really blown it for us with the ultra-conservatives. You remember Mary, my friend from Magdala who had the breakdown? She's here and sends her greetings. Another 'outsider' like us, and 'under the judgment of God'! There are quite a few women following the prophet and you can imagine people think the worst.

You are a remarkable man, husband, to do what you are doing and to allow me this liberty and trust. I wanted to tell you that Jesus has resolved this 'outsider' thing. He is preaching a quiet revolution for us Jews, and the results, I predict (fear), will be cataclysmic. It all makes sense, dear: all of us belong to God; no one is more special; all laws must be tested by the great law of love; religion is not externals but a matter of heart and head. I love it! 'Cataclysmic,' though, because this inclusive doctrine is bound to challenge our old laws and beliefs. Indeed, Jesus recognizes the potential for confrontation. He is saying, new wine for new wineskins. He is saying, sometimes you can't bring the new together with the old (like patching an old coat with new cloth). That's not to say he doesn't try. He wants to 'complete' our history and beliefs and see us fulfilled as a religious people.

If I've got him right, the way he says this can happen is what will unite everyone—Romans, Pharisees, Sadducees, even 'outsiders' —against him. He says he is the representative new person. The old is fulfilled in him. His life is the exemplary one that proves love is the route and destination. Oh, how I want to believe him! I wonder where it will end...

Can I have some more money? Don't know when I'll be home. This is too good to miss and we women (Sue is here as well) are as much part of it as the rest.

Love you,
Joanna

34
THE BOY WITH THE FISHES

John 6:1–15 is the account of the feeding of the five thousand. Statistics abound in this story. One is that it would have taken half a year's pay to feed the crowd one meal (v. 7).

For further reflection or discussion

It is possible that Jesus had moved round the lake close to the town of Bethsaida where Andrew and Philip came from. Both disciples take a part in the story. Andrew, called in Christian tradition the first missionary, brought the boy to Jesus, just as he had brought his own brother (John 1:41). Philip is an intriguing figure who features several times in John's Gospel. He has a Greek name and it is to him that some Greek-speaking Jews say, 'Sir, we wish to see Jesus' (12:21). Here Jesus is testing his faith (6:6), as he was to challenge it subsequently (see 14:8–9).

Feeding the five thousand is the only miracle of Jesus recorded in all four Gospels. Like many miracles, it is multi-faceted. It is a miracle that a boy (a notoriously hungry breed) offers his food. It is a miracle that the poor (barley loaves were their staple) give out of their need. Those who suffer hunger know best what generosity is. It is a miracle of belief, of organization, and of distribution. And it is a miracle reflecting the divine economy: everyone was hungry and then everyone was satisfied.

The monologue asks, what was a boy doing in the crowd?

Was he with his family or did Jesus make such an impact on him that he had to follow and hear more?

Was his spontaneous gift the last, the only food, in the crowd?

Suggestions for staging

A boy on a skateboard, dressed in a modern teenager's clothes.

He can make a play of choosing a postcard from a rack, stamping it and writing it, spelling out the words as he goes.

He whizzes the postcard into a box and rushes off.

LAKE VIEW

Dear Mum,

Auntie Lilith said you'd be worried, so I'm sending you a quick postcard to tell you I'm fine. Do you like the view of the Lake? We all trekked round after Jesus. Catch me walking a hundred metres to hear our rabbi!

Jesus is great. You were right: he should be king. Listen, I know you said, 'One day and straight home', but I'm all right, honestly. Just a bit hungry. You won't believe it, the way you say I eat and eat, but I just donated the rest of your food basket to help feed everyone! There's masses of people here. There were only five barley loaves left, and I wasn't sure about the two fish in this heat. They smelt a bit dodgy. But one of the bodyguards, Andrew, said they should be OK. And he's a fisherman.

Must go. They're saying grace. This is the best gig ever.

Love,
Ben

35

JESUS AND THE SABBATH

John 5:1–18 is the story of the lame man healed in the Bethesda pool on the Sabbath. It is told to show that Jesus looks at people, not at rules. 'The Sabbath was made for man, not man for the sabbath' (Mark 2:27).

For further reflection or discussion

The Gospel of John contains a number of references to the great annual feasts of the Jewish faith. The debate in chapter 5 is about healing on the sabbath, and an extra-special sabbath at that (v. 1).

Water collection under and around the hilly site of Jerusalem played a significant part in its occupation and continuance. In ancient times, the only spring, called Gihon, was outside the city in the Kidron valley. King Hezekiah, in the eighth century BC, brought the water into the pool of Siloam inside the walls by cutting a tunnel nearly six hundred metres long through solid rock.

Great reservoirs have been found under the ancient city. During the 'second temple' period, after the return from exile in Babylon, Jerusalem residents developed these rainwater reservoirs, including the pool called Bethesda. We do not know why it gained a reputation as a spa pool with healing properties. Excavations in the 1960s confirmed that the pool had five porticoes as described by John. It is believed that sheep were washed in one area on their way to the temple for sacrifice. The pool was a considerable size—350 feet long by 200 feet wide and 25 feet deep.

Herod the Great, in the first century BC, built aqueducts on the Roman model to bring water from further sources. In the Bible, 'living water' is a description of springs that did not fail in the summer, and so is used by Jesus to mean that he offers eternal life (John 4:10–15).

Suggestions for staging

The monologue should be delivered by a swimming-pool attendant or someone in caretaker's overalls, holding a mop.

It would help if a temple priest is listening as the monologue is spoken, and reacts accordingly. A priest's dress of the period consists of white, baggy, calf-length trousers, a white robe gathered by a colourful strip of material wound several times around the waist, and a white, conical turban.

The deliberate mixing of costumes is to sharpen the audience's focus on the pool manager's modern preoccupations.

HOPE SPRINGS ETERNAL

Well, it's got to be good for business. My old dad was attendant here before me and, as you know, we have the franchise from the temple. Dad reckoned our job was to keep the pool clean and let you priests worry about the miracles. Or invent them. Can't do any of us any harm.

Some of these characters have been around for years. Members of the family, almost. Jonas was like that. They keep coming, still hopeful. One miracle, just one miracle authenticated by the high priest will keep 'em coming, that's for sure. Well, I mean, what else have they got?

Nope. I've never seen an angel. But call it what you like, this place has got its mysteries. Spooks some people. Travellers come and they say to me they've seen other places like this, where the water suddenly rushes out. Some of these pools work regular as clockwork. I can't explain it, and some things you don't want to, know what I mean?

Anyway, as I say, it gives me a living. The wife and daughters do the refreshments; I do the official guide and bottled water bit. And everyone's happy. Brings out the best in some people, wouldn't you say? Nice to have friends who'll carry you here and stand by you and rush you down into the waters when they're working. It's a good spot. There's shade in the porticoes. It's a bit noisy so near the Sheep Gate, but it means we get the tourist and pilgrim trade.

So about what you're asking. Jonas must be one of our oldest customers. Every day, all weathers, without fail: he's here. Then yesterday—Sabbath, as you know—blow me down, I look up and there he is, walking off cool as a cucumber, with his bed roll. No way is he faking it. He's been around longer than me at the pool. This is a one hundred percent *bona fide* healing miracle, you can tell the high priest.

Oh, and while you're at it, you might ask His Grace for an authentication certificate for us to put up in the cafe. I'm sure he'll be pleased to oblige. Good for business!

36

JESUS THE STORYTELLER

Matthew 22:1–14 and 25:1–13 are two examples of Jesus using weddings as a way of challenging people to be prepared and ready for the Kingdom.

For further reflection or discussion

John the Baptist describes Jesus as the bridegroom (John 3:29). The Church is seen by Paul as Christ's bride (Ephesians 5:29–32). The wedding feast is a vision of perfect joy and communion in heaven (Revelation 19:9).

The custom in the time of Jesus was for the bridegroom to fetch his bride from her parents' home and lead her to his own. As Jesus used wedding metaphors the implications would have been obvious to his hearers: a bridal couple began a new life together; the groom took the bride and made a home for her; old ties were left behind.

The parables of Jesus are always rooted in the everyday life of people. Their characters are farmers and fishermen, kings and merchants, judges and landowners. As a literary form, they are concise and vivid and memorable. Nearly always, Jesus is speaking of 'the Kingdom', that new place or state he calls everyone to enter.

Thus the parable of the marriage feast (Matthew 22:1–14) speaks of God's invitation and humanity's rejection. The wedding garment incident underlines that it is not enough to respond to the invitation: one must be properly prepared. After all, apparently, even wedding garments were often provided for the wedding guests of the period!

The parable of the wise and foolish maidens (Matthew 25:1–13) makes the same point: be properly prepared for the Kingdom. It is not good enough, nor will it work, to rely on others for entry to the wedding reception in heaven.

Suggestions for staging

The monologue introduces the wedding theme and can be performed as a television commercial. Suitable advertising jingle-type music can be chosen.

Miriam can speak from within a cardboard frame, suggesting a TV monitor.

'MAISON MIRIAM'
WEDDING COORDINATION SERVICES

*By appointment, Wedding Coordinator to their Highnesses
the Tetrarch Herod and the Lady Herodias*

Consult me about your wedding theme, colour scheme, stationery, clothing, flowers, ceremony and reception. Let me arrange your marriage from partner to party! My confidential files provide invaluable evidence of potential spouses' orthodoxy, their social and financial standing.

A wide range of liturgies, requisites and all reception requirements removes the anxiety from the mother of the bride. And competitive prices allow the father of the bride to relax and enjoy the whole occasion.

Worried about the groom's friends getting him to the ceremony on time? Or wine running out at the reception? Seeking a source of ready-made colour-coordinated wedding garments? Or needing five or ten virgins with oil lamps? Look no further! Miriam delivers the goods!

Send now for my full price list, with special inclusive offers of tambourines and **FREE OIL!**

37
LEVI AND ZACCHAEUS

Luke 5:27–32 and 19:1–10 describe the calls of Levi and Zacchaeus. Tax collectors were abhorred by the Jews as collaborators with the Roman occupying power. Jesus is more often on the road, in the streets, meeting untouchables, the poor, the alienated, than he is in synagogue.

For further reflection or discussion
Jesus calls sinners to repentance.

His call of Levi (Matthew) cannot have been without prior knowledge of the taxman and some preparation, but it is seen as an abrupt departure by Levi from a lucrative office.

Zacchaeus appears to have enjoyed even more benefit from his job as a chief tax collector, gleaning revenues from a whole district. Jesus names him and invites himself to dinner.

Such public confrontations seem calculated to show the crowds and hostile authorities that Jesus comes not just to all, but especially to the outcasts. It is the more remarkable that some of the Pharisees continued to invite Jesus to dine (Luke 7:36; 11:37), as he had made himself unclean and a dangerous man to know.

Suggestions for staging
The monologue can be delivered by a bright young journalist in city pinstripes, hot from the trading floor.

He can be dictating his story over the telephone, perhaps mentioning punctuation ('new para', 'stop', and so on).

FINANCIAL TIMES—JERUSALEM
SPECIAL PASSOVER EDITION

Following the recent collapse of the House of Levi, another business announced closure at the end of yesterday's trading.

Zacchaeus and Company, based in Jericho, had seemed a rock-solid concern with strong imperial backing and diversifications into traditional city institutions.

As the news broke, it sent shockwaves across the city, still recovering from the previous and equally mystifying Levi crash. With the Passover holiday only days away, the money market needs to make supreme efforts to avoid panic.

Scenes outside the Jericho Head Offices of Zacchaeus last night hardly give ground for early optimism. Long queues of debt claimants were demanding quadruple payments, apparently in response to an extraordinary public offer by the President of the company.

The office of the Procurator is likely to act early today to protect its interests in the lucrative tax operations of Zacchaeus and Company. Assets appear to be dwindling rapidly, our reporter has learned, and a degree of holy glee is manifest in the streets by those who regard the great finance houses as collaborators.

The situation remains unpredictable and precarious as certain political and religious agitators converge on the capital for the coming festival. One at least of these rebel leaders is said to have forged links with both Levi and Zacchaeus.

38
JUDAS ISCARIOT

Matthew 27:3–8 provides the occasion for a sympathetic view of the complications and agonies that bring Judas (or anyone) to betrayal or to suicide.

For further reflection or discussion

Judas Iscariot remains an enigmatic character, condemned as much for betraying his friend (Jesus calls him 'comrade' as Judas kisses him) as for setting unstoppable events in train.

There is an inescapable acknowledgment in the Bible that a Judas is required in the Passion plot. One may echo, 'Woe to the man by whom the temptation comes' (Matthew 18:7) and yet remain stuck with the uncomfortable worry that each of us shares in Judas' betrayal.

In the conclusion, Judas unconsciously touches on the hope of resurrection.

Suggestions for staging

This is a suicide note and needs to be handled with sensitivity.

It could be performed by Judas as he pens it or Peter as he reads it.

Alternatively, it could be performed by an anonymous voice after a suitable introduction.

SUICIDE NOTE

Dear Peter,

When you read this, I'll be dead. But before I go, somehow I just want to try and explain. Not that I really understand myself. I know you must all hate me. It's hard to bear that thought alone, never mind the ghastly rest. We've all shared so much these last years. The band has been closer than brothers and Jesus has brought out the best in each of us.

So why now the worst in me? How could I do it? It's not the money. I admit I enjoy money. But everyone's worth more than thirty pieces of silver.

It's not the political thing. I bet some of you thought I wanted to provoke him into a declaration for an independent Jewish state.

It's not the religious thing, either. I never thought the Messiah was a person. More an idea, I suppose. So I haven't betrayed him for claiming to be anointed, or Son of David.

Betrayed. That word. I can't get round it. I saw your face when I kissed him. I wish I could be like you, Peter. Good old Rocky, like he said. Faithful and steadfast. You'd never betray him, would you? But I'm rambling. Get it over with...

The simple truth is, I can't live up to him. Never could. I've tried and tried. These last dangerous days have really got to me. Believe it or not, I wanted to save him from himself. I meant it to scare him off. I thought he might fade quietly away—go back to the Galilee days, the good times. But now I realize he's too good to live. I should have known that there was no saving him. Now that he's dead or as good as, you should see I've done him a favour—his true friend.

He'll be much greater now he's dead. And I shall be with him.

Judas

39
THE MAID

Mark 14:66–72 is a reminder that Jesus knows each individual so well that he knows what Peter will do when challenged about his allegiance.

For further reflection or discussion

The high priest's house seems to have been used as the setting for the hasty trial and sentencing of Jesus. Some preparations had obviously been set in train should Judas' betrayal be successful. The Sanhedrin had assembled. Its seventy-one members remained the supreme civil and religious court of justice under Roman occupation. Crimes of sedition and treason were reserved to the Roman Governor's judgment and it would appear that he needed to confirm any death sentence.

The Sanhedrin was composed of the temple hierarchy, including serving and past high priests, other chief priests, lay aristocratic elders, and senior religious lawyers known as scribes.

A minimum of two witnesses was required to make an accusation (Numbers 35:30).

Jesus is challenged by the high priest Caiaphas about his claims to be the Christ. Jesus does not deny it but prefers to speak of himself as Son of Man, a title that has both religious and representative meaning.

In this scene, Peter is confronted by a busy maid as he stands on the fringe of the crowd in the courtyard. The maid is probably serving drinks to soldiers clustered around the fire. Peter has dared thus far but his courage fails him when he is asked directly about his allegiance.

Suggestions for staging

The character is a barmaid with a tray of drinks in one hand and a bucket of charcoal in the other.

She addresses Peter as he helps to stack the brazier.

Both are in traditional costume.

THE EDGE OF DENIAL

Here, you! Make yourself useful. Stick this bucket of charcoal on that fire. It's cold tonight; a chill wind that's getting in everywhere.

We could do without all this fuss just before Passover. Couldn't they wait till the new week, these self-important priests and lawyers with their witch hunts? We've got plenty to do just getting things ready for the holiday. I doubt I shall see my bed tonight. There's all the food to prepare and cook. Any number of guests the old man has coming tomorrow and staying over. Beds to make, floors to clean, bread to bake. And you stand here, a great lump, staring—in the way. Get on with you.

Looking at that one, are you? I said he'd come to no good. Been stirring up trouble all week. All year, more like. Ruining everyone's holiday now. A proper nuisance is what he is. Why can't he stay where he belongs, up north? They're all troublemakers up there.

What is it they want, for goodness sake? We've got peace, there's food. Whoever rules, there'll always be taxes. Be content, is what I say.

Have you done yet? Give us the bucket then.

Here. That accent. Just a minute, you're a northerner. You're one of them: a Galilean!

40
THE ROMAN CENTURION

Luke 23:47: an extraordinary verse that has the centurion going beyond admiration for a good and courageous person. He 'praises God' as if realizing that the death of Jesus is for ultimate good.

For further reflection or discussion

Responsibility for any action, any crime, may be shared, but ultimately each individual must take responsibility for his or her own deeds and decisions.

Pilate was the one man who could have stopped the crucifixion if he had wished. His wife had said, 'Have nothing to do with that righteous man' (Matthew 27:19) and Pilate tried, before accepting the will of the mob and washing his hands of the business. Would he have remembered Jesus by the next Jewish Passover, as he himself is remembered in the Christians' creed?

The somewhat biased verdict of two Jewish contemporaries, Josephus the historian and Philo of Alexandria, is that Pilate was more than a weak, vacillating character. He was arrogant, insensitive and savage in his rule—a view that seems to be borne out by his recall in disgrace to Rome in AD36 after the massacre of some Samaritans also caught up in a messianic movement.

Suggestions for staging

The script is read by Pilate in white toga with purple insignia. (*Ave*! and *Salve*! rhyme with 'day,' as 'Ah-vay' and 'Sal-vay'.)

This monologue is to tell us more about the centurion than the procurator. It can be delivered thoughtfully in an aristocratic voice that does justice to the script without necessarily agreeing with it.

THE PROCURATOR, PONTIUS PILATE
FOR YOUR EXCELLENCY'S EYES ONLY

Ave! As requested, I am sending a resume of the Duty Officer's Log for the eve of Jewish Passover, together with these following impressions of a strange and remarkable day.

The Crucifixion Detail was doubled at Your Excellency's desire by the Legate. You pardoned the prisoner Barabbas, leaving three to be executed. The usual scourging was administered and the march to Skull Mound accomplished surprisingly easily. The Nazarene's followers were not much in evidence—mostly a few women. There was never, in my opinion, the least likelihood of armed intervention.

The crowd was hard to read: not as boisterous as the usual holidaymakers; not as ugly as the usual gallows mob. There was more of a watchful, almost I'd say embarrassed, mood—something that was reflected in my squad. I sensed that they had to work themselves up to the execution of this one. The business with the thorn crown and purple toga did not fool me.

We were all sympathetic to this man, and saw him (if I may presume) as I believe Your Excellency did, as a victim of internal religious politics. But these Jews have many such victims and martyrs, Barabbas of course being another. No, there was something else, something more. And that, no doubt, is what Your Excellency requires to know.

He died very quickly and in some pain. The Sanhedrin had obviously arranged their own watch and demonstration. Not very successfully, I thought. You will be aware that I directed them to your office when they protested at your placard saying 'King of the Jews'. They were furious, and all the more determined to have him dead and cleared away. I was pleased to order the despatching of all three wretches before we got too close to sundown. Jesus was already dead.

You will recall it has been a weirdly atmospheric day, with an electric storm circling the city. It seemed to break about the time he must have died. He had said very little. It was his manner.

I found him impressive but I have puzzled how to convey this to Your Excellency. Forgive a plain soldier's simplicity: he seemed to be in charge of the situation. A mad thought, I own. Because here was one weakened by lack of sleep, food and drink. One who had been scourged and made to carry a vast cross. One who had to endure the crowds, the stripping, the nails, all the brutality of our Roman crucifixion. Yet he was looking at me with compassion, right at me. He knew I wasn't in control.

I do not know what else to say that will assist Your Excellency. But this was no criminal, no rabble-rouser, no threat to Caesar. This was a child of God. A good man.

Salve!
P. Justus Flavius, Centurion

41

JOSEPH OF ARIMATHEA

Luke 23:50–53. The character of Joseph is painted as one of integrity. It took courage as a member of the Sanhedrin, the Jewish Council, to ask for the body of Jesus. There was no political or religious advantage in his compassionate act. He was not to know that Jesus would rise from the dead.

For further reflection or discussion

From earliest times Christians have struggled to convey in mere words the mysterious truth that the resurrection of Jesus was an event. The central belief that God had raised Jesus from the dead implies that the first disciples were reacting to something that has much more than an overwhelming sense of the continuity of Jesus' life, much more than group visions of his reappearance.

The empty tomb is a powerful sign and statement that Christ is risen indeed. The evangelists are telling the world, it isn't just a feeling, it's a fact! Yet the dawning realization in the disciples that Jesus has been raised is gradual. His appearances produce an unstoppable but not immediate 'Alleluia!'

The scriptures still convey that breathless awe, that scarcely-daring-to-believe feeling of the first moment, those early days.

As the nascent Church shares its faith and spreads its wings, the resurrection becomes a process. But first and foremost the Gospel is conveying the overwhelming fact that God has acted decisively, at a point in time, through his Son, to rescue, redeem and restore all of humanity.

Suggestions for staging

The scene is a lawyer's office.

The character is an ancient lawyer who is reading his incoming mail.

A sense of puzzlement and mild panic become apparent.

TO COHEN, COHEN AND LEVI, SOLICITORS

16 Fig and Pomegranate Lane
Jerusalem

17th Nissan

Dear Sirs,

I refer to my instructions dated 14th Nissan and sent to you by special messenger.

I realize that the Passover Bank Holiday probably means that such correspondence is only now being processed. I am therefore asking you to ignore my previous letter and regard this communication alone as effective.

I requested you to arrange that the garden cemetery plot marked 'Arimathea' be assigned to Jesus of Nazareth. Burial consent forms were enclosed. Due process of law may not have been followed in this matter because of the need for an immediate burial prior to the Festival.

The grave has now been vacated and has returned to my ownership. If there is any confusion or legal doubt about this new arrangement, please apply in the first instance to the Procurator's Office.

I apologize for any inconvenience.

Yours faithfully,
Joseph of Arimathea

42
MARY MAGDALENE

John 20:15 and 16 describe Mary's encounter with the risen Lord. It is a woman who is the first witness to the resurrection. She fails to recognize him and has to be prompted.

For further reflection or discussion

Simon Peter has found the linen clothes lying in such a manner that the reader is led to believe that Jesus' body has passed from the constraint of clothing whilst leaving the linen graveclothes unwound. His body has not been hidden, stolen or resuscitated. It has been transformed, raised.

There is a gentle disclaimer of Mary's attempt to hold on to the old Jesus, her Teacher, even while Jesus graciously is apparent in bodily form. Here we are invited to stand with Jesus on the brink of eternity and infinity, to view the discarded graveclothes, but also to meet the Gardener, the one who makes all things good and right and restores both humanity and Eden. And when Jesus later meets Thomas, it is to challenge him to a physical response—'Put your finger here, and see my hands; and put out your hand, and place it in my side' (John 20:27) but also to lead him gently on into the larger realm of faith. 'Blessed are those who have not seen and yet believe' (20:29). Jesus' new followers will not need physical proofs, just faith.

Suggestions for staging

The gardener and a companion are having a pint in the local. They can be in modern dress.

The implication is that Jesus is wearing the gardener's overalls and hat when he meets Mary. But it is the whole story, as recounted by the gardener, that is important.

THE GARDENER

Ahh! That's better. I needed that. Same again, please, Miss.

Well it sounds like you had a good holiday, anyway. Wish I could say the same for mine. It's been a nightmare.

Just when I think we're finished and we can lock the cemetery gates, they bring us another body. True! Would I lie to you, my friend? Just on sundown, and our own people too, not Romans. So that makes us ritually unclean for the feast.

I don't know why the army couldn't handle it. It was one of theirs. A convict. Yes, they had an execution on Friday morning. As you say, brilliant timing. Still, I can live with that.

And up to then, it wasn't too bad. It was a bit of a hush-hush job, actually. A friend of one of the Council's, the deceased. And we got well paid to do the necessary. The lads had to stay on to wall up the tomb. Joseph's own it was, too. Whoops! You didn't hear that name. Anyway, it's a massive rock that all six of us have to lever into place.

It's all done, and finally we're going home, when the soldiers arrive. Not there when you need them for the heavy work, of course, but in they march with orders to guard the tomb. I ask you. Who's going to rob a criminal's tomb, even if they can shift the barrier? But, no, they've got orders to seal it and guard it. Good luck to them, if that's what they want to do. Finally, the paperwork is done and we go home.

So we get Saturday, the Passover, off. And no problems. A good time is had by all. Then comes Sunday and the trouble starts. I get a panic message that the tomb has been broken into. So where are the soldiers? Drunk, no doubt. We brace ourselves for a major fuss. Big enquiry. Heads rolling. That sort of stuff. Monday comes, and nothing. Complete silence. Well, not quite complete. The

Superintendent is making more fuss about a set of overalls and a gardener's hat disappearing. Reminds me, I've got to fill in a claims form about it.

So what's going on ? Funny business altogether. Head Office will know, I guess. But the likes of us will never hear the truth of the matter.

Oh, well. Thirsty work. Your round, isn't it?

43
PENTECOST

Acts 2:1–4 is the powerful story of the gift of the Holy Spirit to the disciples on the day of Pentecost. It marks the passing of the old order, shaken to its foundations, and the arrival of the new. It is the birthday of the Christian Church.

For further reflection or discussion

In Acts 1, there is a list of the eleven disciples gathered in the 'upper room, where they were staying' and, significantly, 'with the women and Mary the mother of Jesus, and with his brothers' (1:12–14). This group, it seems, was the inner nucleus of the new believers. A wider group, the brethren, 'in all about a hundred and twenty persons' (1:15), was asked by Peter to vote a successor to Judas Iscariot. Matthias was the one chosen (1:26).

It is not known whether the first group or just the twelve apostles were present on Pentecost Day. It is only presumed that the place they were in was the upper room, but it seems likely. The description of the Pentecost experience mentions Peter and the Eleven (2:14) and refers further to the apostles (2:37, 42). What is certain is that the experience itself was fundamental, earth shattering.

Jewish tradition made Pentecost the anniversary of the giving of the Law, seven weeks after Passover (Leviticus 23:15–21). It was celebrated as Harvest Festival, the feast of Weeks, when the grain harvest was complete and the first new loaves made and offered. John the Baptist had promised a baptism of the Holy Spirit and fire (Luke 3:16). Jesus had said, 'You shall receive power when the Holy Spirit has come upon you' (Acts 1:8). All these combined to grant the disciples, now apostles, the new law, the new message, the new community, the new power—of love.

Suggestions for staging

A modern builder in a flat cap, with a measuring rule and note-pad, is showing the lady of the house through the damaged upper room.

In true builder's style, he plays up the damage but is obviously baffled himself by the cause and extent of the damage.

BUILDER'S ESTIMATE

Must have been some party you had here, Missus. That ceiling ain't just scorched; it's burnt right through. See: here and here and here. There must be a dozen or more great patches. What were you doing? Fire-eating? Downright lethal. Lucky you didn't start a major fire.

Your young man and his friends, was it? You can hardly credit what they get up to these days. I met him on the stairs. Seemed like a quiet young chap. There, you never can tell. If he were mine, I'd really lay in to him.

But that's not the half of it, as well you know. I've worked out an estimate and you are not going to be happy. I'll give it to you straight, you've got major structural damage. Anyone in Jerusalem will tell you we're an honest firm. I'm not talking up the problems. Get a couple more quotes if you like. Doubt whether you'll see fairer. Watch yourself, Missus! That floor could go any minute.

Party, did I say? More like an earthquake. Well, good luck with the assessors, because you're going to need it. No word of a lie, this house has been shaken to its foundations. And how can you explain it? What was it? Rodents? Rot? Upset a few Romans? Someone's started a demolition job, and we might have to finish it. I mean, look at those cracks. Nasty. R-r-r-really nasty.

Tell you what I'll do. I'll send a couple of my fellas to shore you up. I'm promising nothing, mind. Once we start major repair work, you could see whole load-bearing walls coming down. Never seen anything like it in my life. You're not going to forget this in a hurry. I reckon this place will never be the same again.

I can drop in the estimate tomorrow, that suit you?

119

44

SAUL OF TARSUS

Acts 9:23–25 describes the excitement and danger surrounding the conversion of Saul of Tarsus. His ignominious arrival in Damascus as a blind man is equalled by his daring escape over the city walls.

For further reflection or discussion

The impact of Saul of Tarsus' conversion upon the early Church is clear from the three detailed accounts of it in the Acts of the Apostles (9:1–22; 22:4–16 and 26:9–18). The zealous young lawyer, trained by Gamaliel, the foremost legal mind of the day, is at first fanatically opposed to the new religion. Presumably at his own expense, certainly at his own initiative, he equips a touring inquisition, gains the backing of the temple authorities, and rides out to rid the world of Christians.

The famous story records Saul's complete turnaround to the new faith. He was to remain steadfast to it for the rest of his life. His activity and influence in promoting the faith was immense and incalculable.

The episode of the basket underlines dramatically the danger Christians were in and the anger felt at Paul's apostasy.

Suggestions for staging

Ananias should be banging on a door and shouting up at a window in this scene. He wears a cloak and carries a lantern.

BASKET CASE

It's only me—Ananias. Let me in! I'm just on my way to Straight Street to talk to brother Saul of Tarsus. Again.

I know, I know. I felt exactly the same way. How can we believe him? After Stephen and all the others. Is it just an ambitious young lawyer's tricks to trap us all? I say not. Something has happened to him. Something beyond our power or understanding. And anyway, why is he sticking his neck out now and preaching Jesus so openly? You know how the mob is rising. He wouldn't risk death, surely.

We've got to believe him. We've got to help him. Frankly, sister, it would be a good thing if we do get him out of here. He's a liability. Let Peter and the others deal with him.

Just when we were settling down nicely, along he comes like a desert whirlwind. I believe he's genuine. I believe the Lord wants him. I believe he has a job to do. But please, Lord, not here. Not with us. He's a bit too honest and enthusiastic—a bit too dangerous.

Anyway, what I actually came to ask, Doris, is: can I borrow your balcony, a really strong laundry basket and sizeable length of rope, and those four sons of yours? We have a plan to ditch the problem!

45
PETER AND TABITHA

Acts 9:36–42. This and other stories begin to convince Peter that the Church cannot be confined to Jews and Judaism. For the Church, it is a further proof graciously given to Peter of the Lord's resurrection.

For further reflection or discussion

The early chapters of the Acts of the Apostles deal with Peter's adventures. Just before this particular passage there is a delightful phrase: 'Now as Peter went here and there among them all...' (v. 32). He has been exhibiting the signs and wonders of the new age: healing the lame man at the Beautiful Gate (3:2–7), judging the unrighteous Ananias (not the Ananias of 9:10) and Sapphira (5:1–11), preaching in Samaria and confronting Simon the Magician (8:14–24) and finally healing the paralysed Aeneas at Lydda (9:33–34). Joppa was nearby on the coast.

Tabitha, as this monologue tries to show, seems to have been a popular and hard-working servant of the church. Widows had a special place in the pastoral provisions of the early Church, as the detailed instructions of the first letter to Timothy demonstrate (5:3–16).

Why was Peter summoned to Tabitha's deathbed? What was he expected to do? This miracle of bringing life to the dead encouraged the faith throughout Samaria. As Tabitha (Aramaic) was also known as Dorcas (Greek), both names meaning 'gazelle', it is a presumption that she was a Greek-speaking convert. Peter was slowly becoming convinced that the new faith was for no narrow, exclusive group, but for everyone. It is significant that he takes lodgings in Joppa at the house of Simon the Tanner. Jewish law regarded tanning as unclean work.

Suggestions for staging

Tabitha can be late middle-age, wearing a cross, sensibly dressed, a strong, humorous but kindly soul.

Her character needs to come through for this monologue to have authenticity.

TABITHA, RISE

Thank you for inviting me, ladies. I can never resist a quilt-making party, as I think you guessed! I do hope you are not going to be disappointed with my story. I find it hard to tell! It sounds inadequate or incomplete, even to me. I came only because I believe that you, my dear friends, asked me for good and not sensational reasons. I realize you genuinely want to hear from a Christian who has, however briefly, been caught up to heaven. So here I am.

What can I say? I'll tell you what I remember. When you grow older like me, remembering becomes an effort, a selection. Remembering is a way of staying in touch with our little realities and space. Going away and coming back has given me new perspectives. I hope it has made me humble.

Humble but not grateful. There was a fierce protest through my being when Peter brought me back. I'll try to explain.

Those of you who know me well can confirm that I have been very content with my lot. There is nothing I like better than sitting in the upstairs window of my little house, stitching tunics, watching the boats putting out from the harbour. Since my husband's death, my quiet joys have been the sound of seabirds and the sunlight's path on the waters. Joppa and our beloved Plain of Sharon have provided me with the backdrop to my life with you all, in the fellowship of the gospel. I am richly blessed.

God was good. My death was fairly sudden. I had a seizure and can recall a brief struggle before letting go. That feeling! It is impossible to describe. I was falling upwards into a serenity that banished panic. I experienced the lightness of youth again. If I had a body it was supple once more and all my senses heightened. Just like the gazelle, my namesake! I was ready for the adventure to continue. Any fraction of a moment, I just knew I would see, I would understand, I would change.

Voices I recognized were gathering. Then Peter's voice joined in and I was struggling. I had glimpsed, as Lazarus did, that dying was falling in love, finding trustful joy. Peter's act was a tiny part of the continuing miracle of resurrection. And I have become a reluctant witness for you, for others here in Joppa.

So, as I say, here I am. There must be more for me to do. 'Ask Tabitha,' you always say; 'Dorcas will do that.' There must be more squares of the quilt to complete. What I have discovered and freely share with you now, my sisters in the Lord Jesus, is that death is stepping into glory, something to embrace.

For myself, I cannot wait.

46
SIMON PETER

Acts 12:1–11 records the third arrest of Peter. (For the first two, see 4:3–23 and 5:17–25). In this monologue, Peter's release from prison is seen as a type of Christ's resurrection.

For further reflection or discussion

The story of Peter's miraculous delivery from Herod's gaol is one that fires the imagination and has fuelled the faith of countless Christians.

Perhaps this is because of its remarkable and exciting parallels with the story of the resurrection. They are as follows. Herod kills James, as he had killed John the Baptist. Peter, like Jesus, is arrested at the start of the Passover festival. He is put in prison under secure guard, as Jesus was placed in a sealed and guarded tomb.

As the angel of the Lord rolls back the stone door of that tomb, so the angel frees Peter, leading him through doors that open of their own accord. The guards are sleeping or unresisting in both accounts. The angel at the tomb is like lightning in Matthew 28:3, in dazzling clothing in Luke 24:4; and in Peter's cell a light shines out in the darkness.

Peter speaks to the maid Rhoda and at first she fails to recognize him, as Mary Magdalene failed to recognize Jesus. Peter and Jesus both leave a message: 'Tell this to my brothers.' Following Peter's release, as with the aftermath of the resurrection, there was 'no small stir' (Acts 12:18). Finally, Jesus is raised from the dead, and Peter does not escape by himself from prison. He is released.

Suggestions for staging

This is an officer interviewing a subordinate. He wears Roman uniform. This consists of a short, white tunic (an oversized man's shirt will do) with a pleated leather overtunic or breastplate, and helmet. The last two can be made very simply from cardboard and sprayed gold. Alternatively, most toy shops sell realistic plastic armour. The costume is completed with a belt and short sword. If other soldiers are present, they should carry spears, and the officer could wear a red cloak and have a horsehair crest in his helmet.

The officer sits behind a desk and has a paper in his hand which he refers to while addressing the Decurion who may or may not be present and under guard. The Decurion is unarmed.

The officer's tone ranges from sinister quietness to angry incredulity, allowing a final crescendo in the last line.

PETER'S ESCAPE

At ease, Decurion.

Right, I've been through your report and I want to go over some of the details with you now.

Let me see. You transferred from the Cavalry to this unit. I thought that a bit strange, even suspicious, and looked up your records. But I see it was a Jewish girl that prompted that. Still with her? Good. And three children. So, you're a career soldier. Anything for a quiet life, and everything to lose by rocking the boat.

Why, then, do you file this report? Have you gone completely mad? I know we're Herod's guard, but our prime loyalty is still to Rome. This report does not even begin to be a serious, matter-of-fact account of an appalling breach of security. Did you really think you could dish up this sort of bilge and I'd swallow it? A man with your record?

Let's go through this report, point by point. You have sixteen men, four quaternians of soldiers, to guard the prisoner. An important state prisoner. Ringleader of an insurrectionist mob. His capture is a real coup for Herod who wants him kept in maximum security— which we do.

There he is then, this Peter the fisherman, handcuffed to two of your men, locked in a cell, sentries within call, and three heavily guarded gates to get through to escape. Yet escape he does. What is he, then, some sort of magician?

And how does your report explain all this? I quote: 'The prisoner was sleeping between us. He was completely secure. The duty watch were at the alert. A bright light suddenly dazzled us.' Oh, really? What sort of bright light and where did it come from, Decurion? I hardly need to ask, need I? You wrote the report.

'A golden figure appeared in the light and spoke to the prisoner. We were unable to move and the prisoner's chains fell off and the cell door opened by itself. The angel led the prisoner away.'

You've actually come through and said it, soldier. 'The angel.' Do you and your men seriously expect any court-martial to go for that? What do you know about angels, anyway? They're part of Jewish religion, aren't they? I suppose you thought Herod Agrippa would buy that kind of supernatural nonsense, is that it?

Now let me tell you what this is really about, what actually happened back there in the prison. Your wife is one of these terrorists, these Way Followers. She has persuaded you, I don't know how—but you aren't the first or last to be blinded by a woman—to help their leader to escape. You fake the locked handcuffs falling off. You've brought accomplices into the prison. You've lit some Greek fire. You've drugged the other guards!

Well, am I right? I don't know the details. But what I do know is that this is a straightforward escape engineered by you, and you are guilty as hell.

You think you can make a fool of me, of justice? By the gods, Decurion, I should have you crucified for this!

47
BARNABAS AND MARK

Acts 15:37–40 describes the growing pains and personality clashes in the young Church. The leaders debate whether the good news of Jesus is just for Jewish people or is universal (15:22–29). They cannot agree about missionary companions.

For further reflection or discussion

Joseph, a Cypriot Jew, is introduced as 'Son of Encouragement', Barnabas (Acts 4:36). He was a Levite with some property which he donated to the apostles. He became Paul's sponsor, and they worked together in Antioch, where Barnabas was known as a prophet and teacher (13:1).

They set out together on what has become known as Paul's first missionary journey, travelling first to Cyprus, Barnabas' native island. John Mark went with them, but left abruptly to return to Jerusalem (13:13).

The outcome of the tour was to plant churches of mainly non-Jewish members. Upon their return, hostility from Jewish converts against a mission to Gentiles made them journey to Jerusalem to seek support and approval from the Mother Church. A confrontation happened between the Judaizers' party and their own Gentile party. The Judaizers felt strongly that they had enough converted Pharisees (15:5) to make the Church think twice before alienating the Jews. The Gentiles, led by Barnabas and Paul, were able to demonstrate that God was already at work among non-Jews. They believed fervently that the gospel was inclusive and not exclusive. Their views prevailed and they were given the support of the Jerusalem leadership, and a second missionary journey was planned.

It is unclear what precisely the 'sharp contention' (15:39) was all about. Intriguing clues suggest that it was not just over Mark's deserting the original mission. Galatians 2:13 accuses Barnabas of being influenced by the Judaizers' party over a vexed ongoing question of whether Jews could eat with Gentiles.

John Mark is mentioned in 12:12. His home, with its upper room, is believed in tradition to be the place of the last supper and of the coming of the Holy Spirit at Pentecost. Mark 14:51 might provide a biographical clue to the young man's identity as the evangelist Mark. Should this be so, as the monologue presumes, then Barnabas is finding Mark's true role and vocation for him.

Mark seems to have re-established himself in Paul's eyes later in life (see 2 Timothy 4:11).

Suggestions for staging

The monologue picks up Joseph Barnabas' nickname, 'Son of Encouragement' and the description of him as 'a good man, full of the Holy Spirit' (Acts 11:24), by depicting him as a reconciler and encourager.

It perceives him as a man of striking gifts and initiatives but essentially modest. It could be delivered in a warm, persuasive manner. Barnabas can walk about, marshalling his thoughts and arguments.

BARNABAS

Just stop shouting for a minute and listen, will you? Look, I know you're disappointed and frustrated, but Paul's the boss. Right or wrong, he's just taken against you, Mark. No, please listen. It's partly your own fault. You shouldn't have shoved off so abruptly from Cyprus that time. He doesn't trust you...

Now you need to decide. Do you belong back in Jerusalem with Peter and the old gang, or are you coming with me? Let's go back to Cyprus together. You can stay at my place and sort yourself out.

Paul, he can be difficult to work with, heaven only knows, but he means well. Bit intense and single-minded. Besides, he's got this thing about you. After all, you've seen the Lord—known him since you were a teenager. And Paul came late to the faith. He envies you. He can't believe you can be so casual about the gospel. No, I don't mean you are. Of course not. I mean, compared with him, we're a bit laid back, do you see? Now he's very taken with this new chap, Silas. Really keen and anxious to work, he is. Then, I suppose you knew him in Jerusalem?

Anyway, you come with Uncle Barnabas and we'll make a few plans of our own. There's something I've been meaning to suggest. Those stories of Peter's you've got. Perhaps it's time for a proper account. All these new followers—lots of Greeks—they need to know. You could do that, Mark. You could write the story down.

48
LYDIA

Acts 16:14–15. One short cameo picture in Acts opens up intriguing glimpses of Lydia's life and faith. The Church needed her kind of influence, enthusiasm and commitment. Lydia is the first named and notable European convert to Christianity (see Acts 16:9).

For further reflection or discussion

The rag trade must certainly have flourished in a Rome where Messalina was Empress. At the hub of an empire that stretched half across the globe, a richness and diversity of materials and colours were available.

Patrician Romans, both male and female, dyed their hair and sometimes wore wigs. Cosmetics were used on finger and toenails as well as faces. Cassia, cinnamon and balsam were used as body perfumes.

Dress materials were made from silk, linen, wool and woven goat's hair. New cloth was pre-shrunk and soaked in a bleaching agent called 'fullers' earth'. Leather was used for sandals and armour. Dyes were extracted from both animals and vegetables. For instance, saffron and pomegranate gave yellow; woad a bright blue; and from the earth came ochre.

The famous purple dye, the imperial colour, came from the Murex snail that lived in the Mediterranean Sea.

Intriguing glimpses appear in the New Testament of people's daily occupations. 'All of human life' is there! Perhaps not many were wise, powerful or noble (1 Corinthians 1:26), but enough were people of influence, enough with appropriate gifts to move the good news onwards and outwards.

Lydia, a woman of substance and authority because she has her own household (v. 15), meets Paul and Silas at a women's prayer meeting (v. 13). The list of Christian contacts and households in Romans 16:1–16 demonstrates what a wide variety of people received and spread the gospel. Probably most of them remained in their everyday jobs, exercising a quiet yet powerful effect on family, friends and colleagues.

Suggestions for staging

A scatty fashion house designer, overdressed and overacting, delivers this monologue, dashing it off at a keyboard but pausing to leap about a bit in frustration.

PURPLE PASSAGE

Lydia. I'm not getting through to you, am I? Hence this fax. Darling, I need a straight answer. Are you in or out?

Don't, don't go dead on me now. We've built up a marvellous business and frankly, I need your eye and know-how of the rag trade.

Look, we're a brilliant partnership. Think about what we've achieved. Purple, with its imperial monopoly, is the most dangerous, most expensive, most exciting colour for us designers. And we worked darned hard to get the Asian agency, remember? Here I am, stuck with getting the Rome show together in a bare three months and I have nothing, not a toga, not a ribbon, from you. What's happening?

Surely you would have called if the shellfish suppliers had dried up. In any case, I know the Flavian brothers are just as bothered about you. They've been on to me.

There shouldn't be a problem. You have the warehouse full of materials. You have masses of dye. Our biggest market of the year as a fashion house is coming up, and you get religion.

Oh, yes. Don't think the rumours haven't reached here. Sweetie, I know you've always had a bit of a God thing. But isn't this going a bit too far? Get the Galilean out of your system and get back to work. We're depending on you. The whole Imperial Court is depending on you. What can I tell Messalina?

Honest, luvvie, things will soon be desperate. So please, please concentrate. This has got to be your Number One priority.

Fax me back soonest. Love and kisses.
J.

49
PAUL

Acts 27 and 28 need to be read in full, describing the thrills and spills on Paul's final journey to Rome and probable martyrdom. Ironically, if Paul as a Roman citizen had not appealed to have his case heard by the emperor, he might have been freed (26:32). Perhaps he was determined to proclaim Christ from the centre of the known world (see Acts 9:15).

For further reflection or discussion

Whoever wrote the story of Paul's journey to Rome and the shipwreck has made it a gripping yarn. He obviously knew about ships, or made it his business to find out. There is a wealth of nautical detail as well as a swift-moving narrative that suggests the writer was involved personally in the drama. We believe that this was Luke.

The journey probably started in the autumn of AD61, Paul having been kept in prison at Caesarea for about two years, first by Antonius Felix, Procurator of Judea, and then by his successor, Porcius Festus.

Paul had the right as a Roman citizen to trial before the emperor. When Festus wanted to try him in Jerusalem where his enemies were concentrated, Paul appealed to Caesar. Having wintered in Malta after the shipwreck, Paul arrived in Rome in the early part of AD62. Two years of house arrest followed, but Paul was given liberty to preach and teach (28:31).

It was in the winter of AD64–65 that Emperor Nero's persecution of Christians is thought to have included the martyrdom of Paul and possibly Peter.

Suggestions for staging

An excitable little sea captain, jotting vicious notes in a journal.

He ends by watching Paul's approach through his telescope.

It is sadly true that great men are often unapproachable, rude, obsessional, and right! The captain who has lost his vessel cannot bear this.

CAPTAIN'S LOG

Ides of November
in the 815th year from the founding of the City of Rome

We are on the island of Malta and the wretched prisoner Paul safe with us. I loathe that man. I wish I had never sailed from Alexandria. I blame him for the loss of my cargo and my ship. He has a jinx. He is unlucky. The gods shun him!

Worse still, he was right, back in Fair Havens. He said we should winter there. I hate people who are always right. I still say Fair Havens is no place to winter in. We just got unlucky. Or greedy, I suppose.

The centurion is to blame as well. You'd think a member of the Augustan Cohort could make up his own mind. Not Julius. Always listening to Paul. Between them, they practically took over my ship. *My* ship. Captain and owner. A dream come true, owning my own ship. All gone now. A nightmare ship, more like.

The man's a prisoner, for heaven's sake. On trial for his life— bound for the Emperor's Court. Who does he think he is? (*mimics*) 'You should have listened to me.' 'An angel said I would stand before Caesar.' And what happens? We're racing before the wind, no food, near the rocks. The crew try to desert. (Who can blame them?) So we lose a boat. The first disaster. That was Paul interfering. And when we do run aground and the soldiers are going to kill those three, Julius saves them.

So here we are. It's cold. It's raining. Here's me, writing to vent my feelings, and everyone else out in forage parties led by blessed Paul. And here he comes. Wait a minute! He's got a snake on his arm. He's crying out! It's biting him. Yes! There *is* a god!

50
THE LAST THINGS

The book of Revelation speaks of the end of the world in mysterious, beautiful and powerful ways. It talks not only of complete judgment but also of utter bliss.

For further reflection or discussion

Revelation is an extraordinary book. It is apocalyptic literature like the book of Daniel (see Monologue 22) and seems to have been written as a series of visions to comfort and inspire Christians in a time of persecution under the Emperor Domitian (AD91–95).

The visionary John, imprisoned on the Isle of Patmos (1:9), is caught into a vision of the last things. The book is *apocalyptic* because it unfolds a prophetic understanding of history. It draws upon contemporary events but universalizes their significance. That is to say, at one level the book may refer to Roman persecutions but it is equally applicable to any age, to our own.

The book is about *judgment* because it emphasizes that there will come a reckoning for each soul, for the world itself. Oppressors, the immoral, the godless—all will be called upon to answer on the dreadful day (20:12). The plagues (ch. 16) are introduced by a reference to Moses and the Exodus (15:2–4). Just as the plagues inflicted on Egypt long ago were succeeded by the Israelites' salvation, so these plagues are to be the preamble to a new freedom, a new time (21:5).

The book is thus one of *encouragement* that says to Christians in any age, 'Stand firm and all will be well.' Times of testing must be seen within the compass of God's eternal purpose and loving plan.

For the Christian, doomsday is never gloomsday. The book ends with glorious words of hope (22:20). The monologue is couched therefore as a weather forecast—swift, comprehensive and cumulative. It is matter-of-fact, implying, like the book of Revelation, a sense of unavoidable judgment. But the righteous have nothing to fear. As Jesus teaches, his second coming is a time to look up, to lift up heads, for redemption draws near (Luke 21:28). We are left with a picture of Eden restored as a garden city where the tree of life grows; where the gates are open (not guarded by an angel with a flaming sword); where the best of everything continues (21:25–26).

Suggestions for staging

A television weatherwoman describes the calamities using a magnetic board depicting a map of the world and placing appropriate signs and symbols on it as she speaks.

FORECAST

Good evening.

Well, it's been a very mixed bag of weather just lately, with extreme conditions almost everywhere. No place has remained unscathed. The famine and plagues continue unabated and, following the fall of the star, Wormwood, an additional problem seems to have arisen with poisoned seas and lakes and rivers. In consequence, we are experiencing falls of deadly rain in many parts of the globe.

Yesterday's cataclysmic earthquake has seen emergency services out in most major cities. The picture earlier today on the weather charts is just as depressing, I'm afraid. The total solar eclipse was unprecedented and frightening, even awesome. And there is more to come as it seems likely that the moon will turn to blood and many stars could fall.

The upheavals occurring in many parts of the planet are producing some extraordinary phenomena. In particular, the Met Office is warning people to be aware of demonic locust swarms and also a beast that has arisen from the seabed with ten horns and seven heads. The advice is to stay indoors to avoid the worst of the abnormal climatic conditions, such as sores, bloody rivers, scorched earth, and a plague of frogs. These conditions are likely to continue at least through the rest of the night. Troughs of high and low pressure, and both hot and cold fronts, are moving in from the north, south, east and west, and should be with us by morning.

As far as our instruments are registering, significant changes are on the way throughout the planet, and indeed across the universe. My colleagues unite with me in inviting you to stay calm and make what preparations you are able.

A ridge of immense light has already been detected and is gathering in brightness all the time as it moves swiftly in upon us. Very soon, we believe, everyone everywhere will experience the

Son of Man coming on the clouds of heaven with power and great glory. If you look up towards the east, you should get a good view of this.

We understand that following his arrival the situation will change dramatically. The atmosphere will become intensely pure. Sorrow, pain and death will pass away. There will be only great beauty, everyone will be whole and everything will be well.

I think that just about wraps it up. So from me, good night, and God bless you.

PROPER NAMES OF MAIN BIBLICAL
CHARACTERS AND PLACES

SUBJECT INDEX